The Joys of Entertaining

A Party Planner

by Renny Darling

Other Simply Delicious Cookbooks
by Renny Darling

The Joy of Eating
The Love of Eating

Published by Recipes-of-the-Month Club
P.O. Box 5027, Beverly Hills, California 90210
Printed in the United States of America
Library of Congress Catalog Card Number: 78-53363
ISBN: 0-930440-10-2

The Introduction

Entertaining is a world of joys. It is a world of family and friends. It is a time for fun and laughter and sparkling conversation . . . and always, it is a time to enjoy good company, delicious food and excellent drinks. For the hostess, it is a time of excitement and anticipation . . . the stage is set and the curtain is going up on opening night.

Yet, many people, who love *going* to parties and enjoy being with friends, secretly dread the thought of entertaining. The idea of inviting friends for even the most casual dinner leaves them with shivers and shudders.

Let me say, right at the start, that when a party is thoroughly planned to the smallest detail, prepared mostly in advance and staged with glorious food served in an attractive manner, the hostess will feel relaxed and happy and will enjoy her party as much as her guests. Remember, *plan ahead*, *prepare in advance and serve exciting dishes*.

When you entertain with foolproof recipes that are elegant and easy and leave no last minute irritating chores, you *will* feel confident and poised. When you are with your guests for the most part, except for a little visit to the kitchen to pop a dish in or out of the oven, your parties will be great fun for *all* . . . especially you.

The key is plan ahead, prepare in advance and choose an exciting menu. *The Party Plans and Recipes* in this book were designed with this in mind. The recipes were chosen because most of the dishes could be made in advance and heated before serving. Treat yourself to several porcelain bakers that can be used to heat and serve. Once you get used to serving in these, you will never be without them.

Whether you are planning a small dessert or a Bacchanalian repast . . . record it. Jot down the names of those who were invited, who accepted and who declined. Choose guests that you feel will enjoy each other's company. Keep the names, addresses and telephone numbers of your guests in the *Guest Directory* for easy reference. Plan the seating arrangement for optimum compatability.

Choosing the menu takes the most time. Once you have decided on what you are going to serve, the rest is easy. It is simply a matter of following a plan. Write down your menu and next to it jot down the serving pieces. Plan the silver, china, linens, etc. When you feel each item is cleaned or polished and ready to be used, then signal it off on the check list. Again, do as much as possible in advance. This is paramount for your enjoyment of the party. If you leave too many chores for the last minute, you will be harried and nervous. This can make your guests feel uncomfortable and guilty for putting you through so much trouble and it has a dampening effect on the merriment.

Check ingredients needed for the recipes and start the shopping list. If you are planning a visit to the florist or liquor store, note that on the shopping list.

Keep the telephone numbers of bartenders, waitresses, florists, etc. in the handy *Service Directory* provided in the back of the book.

Serve attractively. Decorate and garnish with flair and style. Besides using parsley and green leaves, try flowers, vegetables or fruits. Beautify your home with lots of fresh flowers and candles. All this adds to the spirit of your party and the feeling of hospitality and welcome. It is like saying, "Welcome." or "I'm so glad you could come." or "It's so nice to see you." in just another way.

For, after all, hospitality is the gentle art of pleasing family and friends and it surely follows that it will please you, too.

Enjoy and good luck.

Renny Darling

Renny Darling
Beverly Hills, California
December, 1978

The Contents

For my Debby Darling

who makes every day a party

About this book . . .

The Joy of Entertaining will serve in many ways beyond the planning of your parties. It will act as an *entertaining diary* with a permanent record of all your parties or gatherings. You will know, in a moment, who you entertained, how long ago, what you served, what you wore, etc. It will also serve as a *social handbook* with the directory listing the names, addresses and phone numbers of friends, family, etc. Another feature is the section *Dates to Remember* where you will jot down birthdays, anniversaries or special occasions. All this will add to your "social security."

A handy section is provided to list the local bakeries, liquor stores, florists and the people who provide party services. Include additional recipes on the *Notes* pages provided. Jot down the wines you used and a comment on how much they were enjoyed.

Use the recipes and the menus for parties or family dinners. They represent some very happy memories for me, and I hope they will for you, also.

The Menus and Recipes

An Elegant Champagne Brunch

The Menu

Champagne Orange Punch with Pretty Ice

Shrimp and Crabmeat in Wine with Scrambled Eggs
Apricot Glazed Canadian Bacon
Spiced Apricots

French Mushroom Onion Quiche

Date Nut Muffins
Butter, Cream Cheese, Jams

French Apple Cake
Chocolate Chip Danish Rolls
Coffee

"Come for Sunday brunch . . . and spend the afternoon with us." . . . is a delightful way to entertain friends. Brunch is a leisurely meal that slowly drifts into the afternoon, giving everyone a chance to relax and spend some good time together. Our very lovely champagne brunch should be unhurried, so linger over the strawberry-studded champagne.

Prepare a day in advance every dish except for the scrambled eggs. The cream sauce for this dish can be made a day earlier. Stir in the shellfish and the scrambled eggs just before serving. Have available 2 chafing dishes, one for the eggs and one for the ham or bacon. Set out 1 warmed quiche at a time.

Heat oven to 350° about 30 minutes before serving. Heat the Canadian bacon or ham at the same time with the quiche. Cook the scrambled eggs and place in a chafing dish. Cut and place the French Apple Cake on a footed platter a day earlier and cover it with plastic wrap. Just before the guests arrive, stir the champagne in the punch.

Planning is the key word for our lovely brunch. As guests will usually be arriving around 11, it is important that linen, silver, serving pieces and table decorations be out and ready. Set up as much as possible the day before and leave reheating and last minute touches for the day of your party.

Champagne Orange Punch

2 quarts orange juice
¼ cup lemon juice
¼ cup sugar
orange slices, lemon slices, strawberries
2 bottles (25 ounces, each) champagne, chilled

Combine orange juice, lemon juice, sugar and fruit in a large bowl and refrigerate. (If your punch bowl fits in your refrigerator, then it should be used.) Just before serving, add the chilled champagne and stir. Float the fruit and some Pretty Ice. Serve in a lovely stemmed glass with a strawberry floating on top. Yields 1 gallon punch.

Note – Ways to make Pretty Ice

1. *Freeze 1 quart orange juice in an ice cube tray.*

2. *Place 1 maraschino cherry in each compartment of an ice cube tray, fill with water and freeze.*

3. *Fill a ring mold with strawberries, lemon slices, orange slices or other fruit. Fill with water, cover with foil (to hold fruit down) and freeze. To unmold, dip into water for a few seconds and it will easily slip out.*

Shrimp and Crabmeat in Wine with Eggs

2 tablespoons butter
2 tablespoons flour

¾ cup half and half
1 tablespoon chopped parsley
1 tablespoon chopped chives
6 tablespoons grated Parmesan cheese
2 tablespoons dry white wine

½ pound cooked shrimp
½ pound cooked crabmeat
12 cooked scrambled eggs

Cook together butter and flour for 2 minutes. Add cream, parsley, chives, cheese and wine and cook and stir until sauce is thickened. (Can be made in advance up to this point.) Stir in shrimp and crabmeat. Stir in cooked scrambled eggs. Transfer mixture to a heated chafing dish. Serves 12.

Apricot Glazed Canadian Bacon

2 pounds Canadian bacon or boneless ham round (ready to eat)

½ cup apricot jam
¼ cup honey
1 tablespoon prepared mustard

Combine apricot jam, honey and mustard and heat until blended. Spread mixture over bacon or ham. Bake in a 375⁰ oven for about 30 minutes or until meat is glazed. Cool. Slice thinly, reshape and place in a porcelain baker. Can be prepared a day earlier and reheated at time of serving. Serve garnished with canned spiced peaches or apricots that have been heated with the ham. Decorate with parsley.

French Mushroom Onion Quiche

2 frozen pie shells (9-inch), prebaked in a 400⁰ oven for about 10 minutes or until lightly browned.

4 tablespoons butter
1 onion, finely chopped
½ pound mushrooms, sliced

3 eggs
1½ cups cream
½ cup Parmesan cheese
salt and pepper to taste

Saute onion and mushrooms in butter until onions are tender. Divide mixture between the 2 pie shells.

Beat together the eggs, cream, cheese and seasonings for 2 minutes. Pour mixture evenly into the 2 shells. Place pies on a cookie sheet and bake in a 350⁰ oven for 40 to 45 minutes or until custard is set and top is golden. Serves 12.

French Apple Cake

Crust:
½ pound butter
½ pound cream cheese
2 cups flour
5 heaping tablespoons sifted powder sugar

Beat together butter and cream cheese until blended. Beat in flour and sugar until blended. Roll into a ball, wrap in wax paper and refrigerate for several hours. Butter a 9x13-inch pan. Pat dough on the bottom of the pan. Bake in a 350° oven for 12 minutes.

Filling:
¾ cup apricot jam, warmed
4 or 5 apples, peeled, cored and cut in half vertically. Place cut ends down and cut into very thin slices.

Paint shell with a thin coating of apricot glaze. Line dough with rows of apple slices and bake in a 350° oven for 40 minutes. Baste top with remaining apricot jam and heat in a 400° oven for 10 minutes to set glaze. Serves 12.

Date Nut Muffins

4 eggs, beaten
1½ cups sugar
1 teaspoon vanilla

1½ cups flour
1 teaspoon baking powder
½ teaspoon salt

1 cup chopped walnuts
1 cup chopped dates

Beat eggs, sugar and vanilla for 1 minute. Add flour, baking powder and salt and stir until dry ingredients are just moistened. Do not overmix. Stir in nuts and dates. Spoon batter evenly into 24 paper lined muffin cups. Bake at 400° for 20 or 25 minutes or until a cake tester inserted in center comes out clean. Serve with cream cheese or sweet butter. Yields 24 muffins.

Note – Muffins can be frozen.

Chocolate Chip Danish Rolls

Cream Cheese Pastry:
½ pound cream cheese
1 cup butter (2 sticks)
1 egg yolk
2 cups flour
⅛ teaspoon salt

In the large bowl of an electric mixer, beat together the butter and cream cheese until the mixture is blended. Beat in the egg yolk. Add the flour and beat until blended. Do not overbeat. Turn dough out on floured wax paper. Form dough into a circle, wrap it in the wax paper and refrigerate it for several hours or overnight.

Divide dough in fourths. Roll out one part at a time to measure a 10-inch square. Spread ¼ of the Chocolate Quik over the dough. Sprinkle with ¼ of the chocolate chips. Roll it up, jelly-roll fashion to measure a 10x3-inch roll. Place seam side down on a 12x16-inch teflon-coated baking pan. Repeat with the remaining 3 parts of dough.

Bake in a preheated 350° oven for 30 minutes or until the top is lightly browned. Cool in pan. Cut into slices and sprinkle tops generously with sifted powdered sugar. Yields 24-28 slices.

Chocolate Chip Filling:
16 tablespoons Nestle's Chocolate Quik
8 ounces semi-sweet chocolate chips

Note – A delicious optional is the addition of 1 cup chopped walnuts to the filling. Divide this between the rolls.
– Danish can be frozen after they are baked. Sprinkle with powdered sugar after defrosting.

Indian Curry Buffet

The Menu

Shrimp Curry with Apples and Raisins
Lamb Curry Indian
Chicken Curry with Bananas and Yogurt

Rice India

Peach Lemon Chutney
Apricot Banana Chutney
Apple Orange Chutney
Condiments

Fresh Fruit with Creme Vanilla
Tea Aromatique (with Grated Orange and Lemon Peels)

Pita Bread with Butter and Honey

A curry buffet is easy on the hostess and a delightful way to entertain. Most of the above dishes should be made one day ahead and reheated at time of serving. The chutneys and the Creme Vanilla can be made one week earlier and stored in the refrigerator.

Outside of the rice (which I prefer to make on the day of the party) and slicing the fresh fruit, you can spend the day of your party being nice to yourself, luxuriating in a delicious bath or catching up on some reading.

If you are planning for 20 people the above works well with 3 cups of raw rice (triple the recipe.) Adjust for the number of guests, considering if you are planning dinner, an early supper or simply a light buffet.

All of the recipes can be doubled or halved.

I have not found it satisfactory to freeze.

CONDIMENTS

Chutneys, of course, are always served with a Curry Table. However, do choose at least 4 or 5 of the following:

Chopped chives, sliced cucumbers (very thinly sliced), crumbled bacon (cooked very crisp), coconut flakes, toasted slivered almonds, yellow raisins, peanuts, pine nuts.

Shrimp Curry with Apples and Raisins

1 stick butter
2 onions, finely chopped
2 cloves garlic, put through a press

¼ cup flour
1 tablespoon curry powder (or to taste)
salt to taste

2 large apples, peeled, cored and grated
2 tablespoons brown sugar
1 cup yellow raisins, plumped overnight in orange juice
2 cans chicken broth (10½ ounces, each)

1 pint sour cream
1½ pounds cooked shrimp (medium-sized)

Saute onion and garlic in butter until onions are transparent. Add flour, curry powder and salt and cook for two minutes stirring all the while.

Add apples, brown sugar, raisins and chicken broth. Cook over low heat, stirring, until sauce thickens. (If sauce is too thick, add a little more broth). Stir in sour cream and shrimp and heat through. Do not allow to boil. Serves 6.

Note: – Dish can be prepared a day earlier up to the point of adding the sour cream and shrimp, which should be done before reheating. Heat through and do not allow to boil.

Lamb Curry Indian

3 pounds lamb (use a leg of lamb), have butcher cut the meat into ½-inch cubes. Sprinkle with salt to taste.

2 cups onions, finely chopped
½ cup butter (1 stick)
6 cloves garlic, mashed

1 can (1 pound 12 ounces) tomatoes, drained. Reserve juice for another use. Chop coarsely.

1½ teaspoons tumeric
1 teaspoon curry powder
½ teaspoon crushed red hot chili peppers
1 cup golden raisins

1 cup toasted slivered almonds

Saute onions in butter until onions are soft. Add garlic and lamb and cook, tossing and turning until lamb is lightly browned.

Add tomatoes, tumeric, curry powder, crushed peppers, and raisins. Cover and simmer until lamb is tender, about 45 minutes.

Add almonds before serving. Serves 6.

Note: – This dish should be made 1 day ahead and refrigerated to allow flavors to blend. Remove from the refrigerator and reheat over a low flame.
– Serve with Rice with Onions.

Rice India

1 cup long grain rice
2 tablespoons butter
1 can (10½ ounces) chicken broth
1 cup water
½ teaspoon tumeric
salt and pepper to taste
1 onion, finely chopped
2 tablespoons butter
½ cup toasted slivered almonds

In a saucepan, combine rice, butter, chicken broth, water and seasonings. Stir, cover and simmer mixture until liquid is absorbed and rice is tender, about 30 minutes.

Meanwhile, saute onion in butter until it is soft. When rice is cooked, stir in the onion and slivered almonds. Garnish with finely minced green onions. Serves 6.

Chicken Curry with Bananas and Yogurt

3 cups cooked chicken, diced

2 onions, finely chopped
1 clove garlic, mashed
4 tablespoons butter

2 tablespoons flour
1 teaspoon curry powder (or more to taste)
1 teaspoon tumeric
1 tablespoon brown sugar
1 cup chicken broth

1 cup yogurt
3 sliced bananas, tossed in lemon juice (about 1 or 2 teaspoons lemon juice)

salt to taste

Saute onion and garlic in butter until onion is soft but do not brown. Add flour, curry powder, tumeric and brown sugar and cook and stir for a minute or two. Add chicken broth and cook and stir until sauce thickens. If the sauce is too thick, add a little broth.

Add yogurt and bananas and stir and heat through. Now add the cooked chicken and heat through. Serve with rice. Serves 5 or 6.

Note: – Entire dish can be assembled and made a day earlier up to the point of adding the bananas and yogurt which I would add when reheating before serving.

Apricot and Banana Chutney

½ pound dried apricots
1 cup apricot nectar

2 cups sugar
½ cup vinegar
½ cup apricot nectar
1 cup, scanty, black currants
3 bananas
½ teaspoon ground ginger
pinch of garlic powder

Cook together the apricots and the apricot nectar until the apricots are soft and nectar is absorbed. Set mixture aside.

In another saucepan, combine sugar, vinegar and ½ cup apricot nectar and cook until mixture is syrupy. Candy thermometer should register about 230^{0}.

Now, add the apricots to the syrup along with the remaining ingredients and cook for another 15 minutes over low heat, stirring now and again. Be careful not to scorch the apricots.

Cool chutney in pan and then place in a jar, cover and refrigerate. Makes about 2 cups.

Apple Orange Chutney

1½ cups sugar
½ cup brown sugar
¾ cup vinegar
1 cup orange juice
2 oranges, grated. Use fruit, juice and peel. Remove any large pieces of membrane.
3 apples, peeled, cored and grated
½ teaspoon ground ginger
1 cup golden raisins

Combine all the ingredients in a large saucepan and stir to mix well. Cook, over medium heat until mixture is syrupy and candy thermometer registers around 230°. Allow mixture to cool and then store in a jar, cover and refrigerate. Makes about 3½ cups chutney.

Peach Lemon Chutney

1 can (1 pound 12 ounces) sliced peaches
1 cup yellow raisins
2 cups brown sugar
2 lemons grated. Use peel and fruit. Remove any large pieces of membrane.
1 cup walnuts, coarsely chopped
½ cup vinegar
pinch garlic powder
pinch of salt
½ teaspoon ground ginger
½ teaspoon cinnamon

Combine all the ingredients in a saucepan and cook over medium heat until mixture is syrupy and candy thermometer registers about 230°. Allow mixture to cool and then store in a jar, cover and refrigerate. Makes about 3½ cups chutney.

Note: - These chutneys are exceedingly delicious and can be used as a spread on bread with sweet butter.
- Chutney can be made several weeks before your party.

Tea Aromatique

To 2 ounces of Spiced Tea, add 1 tablespoon grated orange peel and 1 tablespoon grated lemon peel. Toss the tea and the peels together and place in a tightly covered jar. If you are extra adventuresome, add a little cinnamon.

Pita Bread with Butter and Honey

With a scissor, trim off the edge of the pita bread about ⅛-inch. You will have 2 flat circles of bread. Cut each half in quarters, spread with sweet butter and honey. Sprinkle with a few sesame seeds. Broil for a few seconds only. Bread should not brown, but will be very crisp. Make about 10 pitas for 20 people.

Fresh Fruit with Creme Vanilla

Arrange an attractive platter of varied fresh fruit; melons, papayas, mangos are especially nice. Strawberries, bananas, oranges are good too. Place a bowl of Creme Vanilla close by for spooning over the fruit.

Creme Vanilla

1 cup whipping cream
½ cup sour cream
1 tablespoon sugar
1 teaspoon vanilla

In a glass jar, mix the creams together until well blended. Leave the jar uncovered and at room temperature for about 4 hours or until the cream has thickened. Stir in the sugar and vanilla. Cover and refrigerate. Makes about 1½ cups Creme Vanilla.

Note: - *This is an incredibly delicious sauce. You will enjoy using it over fresh fruit. It is also very good over puddings or pies. A tablespoon or two, spooned over dessert will transform a quite ordinary dessert into a culinary delight.*
- *Creme Vanilla will keep, refrigerated, for at least 1 week.*

An Italian Feast

The Menu

Scampi with Shallots, Garlic and Lemon Sauce
Crusty Italian Bread

Osso Bucco alla Milanese
Buttered Peas with Shallots and Parsley
Risotto alla Milanese
(Rice with Parmesan)

Heavenly Chocolate Ricotta Cheesecake
Cafe Espresso

This is a wonderful dinner to consider some frosty evening when you are dining informally with family or friends. While it is certainly very appealing for youngsters and grown-ups alike, the men seem to especially love these stout-hearted and robust dishes. For some reason, they are so delighted to soak up the garlic sauce with the crusty Italian bread. And then, with much gusto, they pick the meat off the veal shanks and scoop out every last morsel of marrow.

In addition, the dinner is a delight to prepare and very easy to serve. All the dishes can be prepared a day earlier, with the exception of the shrimp (which can be assembled 30 minutes earlier.) Have the shrimp ready, the sauce assembled and then broiling is just a matter of minutes.

The veal shanks should be prepared a day earlier to allow the flavors to blend. The cheesecake is also better when refrigerated overnight.

Cafe Espresso is made with very finely ground Italian coffee, and is served in a demi-tasse or Espresso glass. In the absence of an Espresso coffee maker, you can purchase Instant Espresso in gourmet markets. Traditionally served with a twist of lemon peel, I very much prefer the addition of a dash of Kahlua Coffee Liqueur and a dollup of whipped cream.

Scampi with Shallots, Garlic and Lemon Sauce

1½ pounds large shelled shrimp, peeled and deveined

½ cup butter, melted
¼ cup olive oil
4 cloves garlic, put through a press
3 shallots, finely chopped
3 tablespoons lemon juice
3 tablespoons minced parsley
Salt and freshly ground pepper to taste

Place shrimp in an 8 or 9-inch pan. Combine the remaining ingredients and toss to blend them thoroughly. Pour sauce over the shrimp, making certain that the shrimp are well coated.

Broil shrimp about 6-inches from the heat, a few minutes on each side and only until shrimp turn pink and become opaque. Watch carefully so that the shrimp are not over-cooked. Serve at once with the sauce spooned over the top. Serves 6 as a first course, or 4 as a main dish.

NOTE: – *Perhaps one of the easiest and best ways to prepare shrimp is to broil them for a few minutes in a rich garlic, butter and lemon sauce. Serve this with a loaf of crusty Italian bread to dip in the heavenly sauce.*
– *Sauce ingredients can be mixed together earlier in the day. Entire dish can be assembled 30 minutes before broiling. Broil just before serving.*

Osso Bucco alla Milanese

Try this marvelous recipe one night soon. It is such fun to pick the meat off the bones and scoop out every little morsel of marrow.

3 veal shanks (also called shinbones) about 6 pounds. Ask butcher to saw them into 3-inch pieces. Sprinkle them with salt and pepper and dust them lightly with flour.

6 medium onions, cut into fourths

2 cans (1 pound, each) stewed tomatoes, chopped. Discard seeds.
1 can (8 ounces) tomato paste
1 cup dry white wine
2 teaspoons beef stock base
1 carrot, finely grated
1 tablespoon sugar
3 tablespoons olive oil
4 cloves garlic, put through a press
½ teaspoon each, oregano, basil and thyme or 1½ teaspoons Italian Herb Seasoning
salt and freshly ground pepper to taste

Place veal shanks in a 12x16-inch roasting pan marrow side vertical. Scatter onions evenly over all.

Stir together the remaining ingredients until the mixture is blended and pour sauce evenly over the veal. Cover pan tightly with foil and bake in a 350° oven for about 2 hours or until veal is tender. Sauce should be quite thick, vegetables tender and the aroma will fill your house with family and friends. Serve with Risotto alla Milanese (which is the traditional accompaniment to this dish) or a lovely Light Tomato Rice. Serves 6.

NOTE: – *Best made a day before to allow flavors to blend.*
– *Just before serving you can sprinkle a little Gremolada over the veal. This consists of 1 tablespoon grated lemon rind, 3 tablespoons chopped parsley, 1 clove garlic, minced and 1 anchovy mashed.*

Buttered Peas with Shallots & Parsley

2 packages (10 ounces, each) frozen peas
¼ cup butter
3 shallots, finely chopped
½ teaspoon sugar
3 tablespoons finely chopped parsley
salt and pepper to taste

Combine all the ingredients in a saucepan and over low heat, slowly saute vegetables until peas are tender but firm. Serves 6.

NOTE: – *Entire dish can be prepared earlier in the day and refrigerated. Reheat before serving.*

Risotto alla Milanese
(Rice with Parmesan)

4 tablespoons butter
1 small onion, finely chopped
1½ cups rice

2 cans (10½ ounces each) chicken broth
½ cup water
salt and pepper to taste
pinch of saffron softened in 2 tablespoons water
4 tablespoons grated Parmesan cheese (or more to taste)
2 tablespoons melted butter

Saute onion in butter until onion is soft. Add rice and saute for 2 minutes, stirring and turning. Carefully add broth (it will splatter for a few seconds) and water and stir. Stir in salt and pepper. Cover pan and simmer rice for about 30 minutes or until rice is tender and liquid is absorbed. Stir in saffron, cheese and melted butter and continue cooking for about 5 minutes. Serve with Osso Bucco. Serves 6.

Pink Rice in a Light Tomato Sauce

1 can (10½ ounces) chicken broth
¾ cup water
3 tablespoons butter, melted
salt and pepper to taste

1 tomato, peeled, seeded and chopped (or 1 canned tomato, chopped)
2 tablespoons tomato sauce
1 tablespoon chopped parsley
1 tablespoon chopped chives

1 cup rice

Combine all the ingredients in a saucepan and stir until mixture is blended. Cover pan and simmer rice until it is tender and liquid is absorbed, about 35 minutes. Serve with chicken or veal, Italian style. Serves 4 or 5.

Heavenly Chocolate Ricotta Cheese Cake

If you are a chocolate fiend, as you know I am, I know you will enjoy this rich and glorious chocolate cheesecake.

CRUST:
1 cup chocolate wafer crumbs
⅓ cup butter, melted
½ cup finely chopped walnuts

Combine crumbs, butter and walnuts and mix until blended. Press the mixture on the bottom of a 9-inch springform pan.

FILLING:
¼ cup cream
8 ounces semi-sweet chocolate chips

1 pound Ricotta cheese, at room temperature
½ pound cream cheese
1 cup sugar
3 eggs, at room temperature
1 cup sour cream, at room temperature
2 teaspoons vanilla

In a small saucepan heat the cream. Add the chocolate chips and stir until chocolate is melted. Do this over low heat so that you do not scorch the chocolate. Set aside.

Beat together the Ricotta, cream cheese, sugar, eggs, sour cream and vanilla until the mixture is thoroughly blended. Beat in the melted chocolate. Pour cheese mixture into the prepared pan and bake in a 350° oven for about 55 minutes, or until a cake tester inserted in center comes out clean. Do not overbake. Allow to cool in pan and then refrigerate for 4 to 6 hours. Overnight is better. Garnish top with lots of chocolate curls. Remove from the refrigerator 20 minutes before serving. Serves 12.

NOTE: - To make chocolate curls, take a vegetable peeler and run it down the sides of a chocolate bar that is at room temperature.
– Get ready for a standing ovation.

A Greek Peasant Dinner

The Menu

Greek Salad with
Creamy Lemon Dill Dressing or
Lemon Dill Vinaigrette

Sesame Bread or
Flaky Filo Cheese Triangles

Moussaka
(Eggplant Casserole with Meat Sauce and Cream Topping)

Herbed Rice with Tomatoes and Onions

Baklava
Greek Coffee

Some cold, wintry night you would do well to consider this menu, with a Greek theme, for an informal dinner with family or friends. The dishes translate well to American tastes. The menu is especially easy on the hostess, for all of the dishes, except the salad, can be prepared a day earlier and reheated at the time of serving.

The salad could be made simply with lettuce, tomatoes, cucumbers and green onions, but with the addition of olives and feta cheese, it will feel more like a party. The sesame bread can be purchased at a Middle Eastern grocer. In the absence of one, a French bread, generously sprinkled with sesame seeds, would be an acceptable alternative. The Filo Cheese Triangles, served hot, with the salad (instead of the bread) are a delicate and memorable optional. These, too, can be prepared a day earlier and reheated at time of serving.

Moussaka is a classic Greek dish and the elegant version given here will appeal to those who are counting calories, for the eggplant is steamed and not sauteed in oil. You can use ground beef or ground lamb for this recipe. Using half lamb and half beef also works very well.

Herbed Rice with Tomatoes and Onions is a fine accompaniment. I recommend that you allow for extras, as the men usually go overboard with this dish.

Dessert, the very exciting Baklava, can be made several days earlier. If you are serving the Cheese Triangles, then serve the marvellous Greek Honey Nut Cake as an alternative. Greek Coffee should be served very strong and sweet and in demitasse cups.

Greek Salad
with Creamy Lemon Dill Dressing

4 cups cut lettuce
4 medium tomatoes, cut up
1 large cucumber, peeled and cut into thin slices. (If you have a few extra seconds, run a fork down the peeled, cucumber and then, when it is sliced, the edges will have a pretty decorated look.)
¼ cup pitted olive slices
4 ounces feta cheese, crumbled
3 green onions, finely chopped
2 tablespoons chopped parsley
salt and freshly ground pepper to taste
2 anchovies, mashed (optional)

Combine all the ingredients in a large salad bowl and toss to mix. Pour Creamy Lemon Dill Dressing over the salad just before serving and toss to coat evenly. Serves 6.

Creamy Lemon Dill Dressing

1 cup sour cream
½ cup cream
3 green onions
3 tablespoons lemon juice
½ teaspoon dried dill weed
⅛ teaspoon garlic powder
1 teaspoon sugar
4 sprigs parsley, remove twigs
salt and pepper to taste

In a blender or food processor, place all the ingredients and blend until the dressing is flecked with green. Store dressing in a jar with a tight fitting lid. Refrigerate until serving time. Yields 1¾ cups dressing.

Greek Salad
with Lemon Dill Vinaigrette

This is a delicious alternative dressing for the Greek Salad.

Lemon Dill Vinaigrette

¼ cup lemon juice
1 tablespoon wine vinegar
1 tablespoon water
¾ cup oil
½ teaspoon dill weed
1 clove garlic, put through a press
2 tablespoons grated Parmesan cheese
salt and pepper to taste
1 tablespoon minced parsley

Place all the ingredients in a jar with a tight fitting lid and shake vigorously until the mixture is well combined. Refrigerate dressing until serving time. Yields about 1 cup dressing.

Flaky Filo Cheese Triangles

½ pound filo leaves (purchased at a Middle Eastern grocery)
1 cup grated feta cheese
½ cup cottage cheese
¼ pound cream cheese
2 eggs

melted butter (about ½ pound)
grated Parmesan cheese

Cut filo leaves in strips to measure about 14×3-inches. Beat together the cheeses with eggs until the mixture is blended. Working one strip at a time, brush filo leaf with butter. Place 1 teaspoon cheese mixture on one end. Pick up one corner and cover filling forming a triangle. Fold triangle over and over to the end of the strip. Brush triangle with melted butter. Repeat for remaining strips. Sprinkle tops with grated Parmesan cheese.

Place buttered triangles on a baking pan and bake in a 350° oven for 20 minutes or until golden brown. Serve with soup or salad. Yields 36 pastries.

NOTE: – Pastries should be reheated before serving to crispen leaves.

Moussaka

(Eggplant Casserole with Meat Sauce and Cream Topping)

2 eggplants, peeled and sliced into ½-inch thick slices

Sauce:

4 cups chopped onions
¼ cup butter
2 pounds ground beef or ground lamb
3 tablespoons dried parsley flakes
1 can (1 pound) stewed tomatoes, chopped
1 can (8 ounces) tomato sauce
¼ teaspoon garlic powder
salt and pepper to taste

Cream Topping:

1 pound Ricotto cheese
½ pound cream cheese
3 eggs

Crumb Mixture:

1 cup bread crumbs
1 cup grated Parmesan cheese

Place eggplant slices in a greased 12×16-inch pan. Cover pan tightly with foil and cook eggplant in a 400° oven for 20 or 25 minutes or until eggplant is soft.

In a large skillet, saute onion in butter until onion is soft. Add ground meat to skillet and saute until meat loses its pinkness. Add the remaining sauce ingredients and cook it for 5 minutes.

Beat together the Ricotto cheese, cream cheese and eggs until mixture is blended.

Combine bread crumbs and grated cheese.

In a 9×13-inch pan, spread a little sauce. Layer ½ the eggplant slices, ½ the sauce and ⅓ the crumb mixture. Repeat with the remaining eggplant, sauce and ⅓ the crumb mixture. Spread Cream Topping evenly over the top and sprinkle remaining crumb mixture over all. Bake in a 350° oven until piping hot and crumbs are lightly browned, about 35 minutes. Serves 6 to 8.

Herbed Rice with Tomatoes and Onions

1 onion, finely chopped
2 tablespoons oil
1 cup long-grain rice

1 can (10½ ounces) chicken broth
¾ cup water
1 tomato, peeled, seeded and chopped
2 tablespoons tomato sauce
2 tablespoons chopped chives
2 tablespoons chopped parsley
salt and pepper to taste
pinch of thyme

Saute onion in butter until onion is soft. Add rice and saute until rice is just beginning to color. Stir in the remaining ingredients carefully, cover and simmer rice until liquid is absorbed and rice is tender, about 30 minutes. Serves 6.

Greek Coffee

In a saucepan or brass Greek coffee brewer, bring to a boil 2 cups water, 6 cubes sugar and 6 teaspoons pulverized ground coffee. Stir briskly and remove from heat. Wait for a few seconds to allow coffee grounds to settle and pour coffee into demitasse cups. Yields 6 cups.

The Easiest and Best Baklava

Baklava is known the world over as one of the most majestic and exotic desserts. Actually, it is very easy to prepare. It is important that you have all the ingredients assembled in advance and then you will be assured of perfect results every time.

Syrup:

1½ cups sugar
1 cup water
½ cup honey
2 tablespoons lemon juice

Cook together the sugar, water and honey and simmer the mixture for 15 minutes or until it is syrupy. Add lemon juice and set aside to cool.

Nut Mixture:

1 pound walnuts, coarsely grated. (If you use a food processor, use the steel blade for a few seconds.)
¾ cup sugar
3 teaspoons cinnamon

Combine nuts, sugar and cinnamon and mix thoroughly.

Basting Mixture:

1 cup butter (2 sticks), melted
½ cup oil

Combine butter and oil and stir until blended.

Filo:

1 pound filo (strudel) leaves

Have syrup, nut mixture, basting mixture and filo leaves ready. Brush a 9x13-inch pan with basting mixture. Now start layering in the following order. Place 2 filo leaves in pan. Sprinkle 6 tablespoons nut mixture evenly over top. Place 1 filo leaf over the nuts. Baste this one generously with basting mixture. Cover with 1 filo leaf. Sprinkle with 6 tablespoons nut mixture. Alternate layers in the same fashion, 1 filo leaf, basting mixture, 1 filo leaf, nut mixture until the nuts are all used up. Place 2 filo leaves over the top. Cut the Baklava into diamond shapes. Sprinkle top with 3 tablespoons sesame seeds. Bake in a 350° oven for 40 minutes or until top is a golden brown. Remove from oven and immediately pour the cooled syrup evenly over the top. Allow to cool in pan. Serves at least 12.

Greek Honey Nut Cake

3 eggs
¾ cup sugar

2 cups Ritz cracker crumbs (about 42 crackers)
¾ cup sugar
1 teaspoon baking powder
1 teaspoon cinnamon
1 teaspoon vanilla
1 orange, grated (remove any large pieces of membrane)
1½ cups chopped walnuts

Beat eggs with ¾ cup sugar until eggs are very pale, about 5 minutes. Beat in the remaining ingredients until they are blended.

Pour mixture into a lightly buttered 9-inch spring-form pan and bake at 350° for 30 minutes. Remove cake from oven and pour Honey Cinnamon Syrup over it. Cool cake in pan and serve in wedges. Serves 8.

Honey Cinnamon Syrup

⅔ cup sugar
⅔ cup water
⅓ cup honey
1 slice lemon
1 cinnamon stick

Cook together all the ingredients until mixture is syrupy, about 15 minutes. Remove lemon and cinnamon stick. Allow to cool. Pour syrup over cake.

A Sunday Night Family Dinner

The Menu

Green Salad with Italian Herb Dressing
or
Mushroom Cucumber Salad with Garlic Anchovy Dressing

Garlic Cheese Lemon Bread

Stuffed Chicken Romano with Garlic Butter Lemon Sauce
Italian Green Beans with Butter and Onions

Spaghetti alla Bolognese
or
Fettucini with Zucchini

Tartufo alla Tre Scalini Caffe

This is a lovely dinner when you are having friends or family for a casual Sunday meal. Plan a salad to the taste and appetites of your company. The Green Salad is light and the Mushroom Cucumber Salad is a little more filling, but both very good with the Garlic Cheese Lemon Bread. The salad will be made on the day of the dinner but the dressings can be made 1 week earlier.

The Stuffed Chicken Romano will be rolled in the morning, refrigerated in its baking pan and will be popped into the oven 1 hour before serving. Vegetables can be made earlier in the day and reheated at time of serving. Spaghetti sauce can be made several days earlier and stored in the refrigerator. Spaghetti will be made later in the day. It can be cooked earlier in the day and tossed with some oil to prevent sticking. Then you only need to plunge it into boiling water for 2 minutes and then drain and serve. A spaghetti cooker is a must for this. If you are having young children, I recommend the spaghetti. The Fettucini is a better dish for adults.

Of course, everybody will love the Tartufo and keep the cherries in the center as a surprise.

Italian Herb Dressing

This simple little dressing is especially good over an antipasto or mixed green salad.

½ cup oil
¼ cup olive oil
¼ cup red wine vinegar
1 shallot, minced
1 teaspoon oregano
1 teaspoon sweet basil
¼ teaspoon thyme
2 cloves garlic, put through a press
salt and freshly ground pepper to taste

Combine all the ingredients in a glass jar with a tight fitting lid and shake vigorously until blended. Refrigerate until ready to use. Yields about 1 cup.

Note – If the dressing needs a little sweetening, use ½ teaspoon of honey or sugar.

Garlic Anchovy Dressing

If you feel like going overboard, try this delicious dressing over a salad made with mushrooms, cucumbers, onion rings, radishes and mixed greens.

½ cup oil
¼ cup olive oil
¼ cup lemon juice
2 anchovy fillets, mashed
2 tablespoons chopped chives
2 cloves garlic, put through a press
½ teaspoon Dijon style mustard
2 tablespoons grated Parmesan cheese
salt and pepper to taste

Combine all the ingredients in a glass jar with a tight fitting lid and shake vigorously until blended. Refrigerate dressing until ready to use. Yields about 1 cup.

Note – Both dressings can be stored for 1 week in the refrigerator.

Garlic Cheese Lemon Bread

1 loaf Italian bread, cut in half lengthwise.

½ cup olive oil
2 cloves garlic, put through a press
½ cup grated Parmesan cheese
2 tablespoons lemon juice
paprika

Combine olive oil, garlic, cheese and lemon juice. Spread this mixture on the cut surfaces of bread. Sprinkle top with paprika. Broil for a few minutes or until top is lightly browned. Serves 8.

Italian Green Beans with Butter and Onions

2 packages (10 ounces, each) Italian Green Beans
¼ cup butter
2 tablespoons dried onion flakes
salt and pepper to taste

Cook vegetables according to directions on the package until tender but firm. Drain and refresh in cold water.

Meanwhile, heat butter and saute onion flakes until they are slightly colored. Add the green beans and continue sauteing until beans are thoroughly coated with butter mixture and are tender. Serves 6.

Note – Entire dish can be made earlier in the day and refrigerated. Reheat before serving.

Stuffed Chicken Romano with Garlic Butter Lemon Sauce

8 half chicken breasts, boned, skinned and gently pounded to flatten. Sprinkle with garlic powder.
8 thin slices prosciutto ham
8 thin slices Mozzarella cheese

Place one slice of ham and cheese over each half of breast. Roll up and secure with toothpicks. Roll chicken in Seasoned Bread Crumbs and place in a baking pan.

Bake in a 325° oven for 20 minutes. Baste with Garlic Butter Lemon Sauce. Continue baking and basting for another 30 minutes (use all the sauce) or until chicken is cooked. Serve at once. Serves 8.

Seasoned Crumbs:
¾ cup bread crumbs
¼ cup flour
½ cup grated Parmesan cheese
2 teaspoons garlic powder
2 teaspoons paprika
1 teaspoon salt

Combine the ingredients in a jar and shake until blended. Store unused crumbs in the refrigerator. Can be kept for several months and very good to have on hand to use with fish or chicken.

Garlic Butter Lemon Sauce:
½ cup butter (1 stick)
2 cloves garlic, put through a press
2 tablespoons lemon juice
1 teaspoon parsley flakes

Heat together all the ingredients until butter is melted. Use to baste chicken. Yields about ½ cup sauce.

Note – Entire dish can be assembled earlier in the day and refrigerated. However, I would recommend that you bake it just before serving.

Spaghetti alla Bolognese

(Spaghetti with Meat and Tomato Sauce)

This rich and flavorful meat and tomato sauce is probably one of the best loved sauces in all Italy. It can be used over veal, eggplant and various pastas.

1 onion, finely chopped
½ cup finely grated carrots
3 cloves garlic, minced
2 tablespoons butter
2 tablespoons olive oil

1 pound lean ground beef

2 cans (1 pound, each) stewed tomatoes, finely chopped
1 can (8 ounces) tomato paste
½ cup dry white wine
4 tablespoons minced parsley (or 2 teaspoons dried parsley flakes)
2 teaspoons Italian Herb Seasoning (or 1 teaspoon oregano and 1 teaspoon basil)
1 bay leaf
2 teaspoons sugar
salt and freshly ground pepper to taste

In a Dutch oven or large saucepan, saute onion, carrots and garlic in butter and olive oil until the vegetables are soft. Add the ground beef and continue sauteing until the meat loses its pinkness.

Add the remaining ingredients and stir until the mixture is well blended. Simmer the sauce, uncovered, for about 40 minutes. Remove bay leaf and adjust seasonings. Serve with pastas, chicken, eggplant or veal. Yields about 1 quart sauce, enough for about 1 pound of spaghetti.

How to Cook Spaghetti

I like using a spaghetti cooker for pastas. It facilitates draining and can be used to keep the pasta warm for a short while. In absence of this, use a large pot, allowing about 3 quarts of water for each pound of pasta. Add 2 tablespoons oil to the water to help prevent pasta from sticking. Bring water to a boil, add 3 teaspoons salt, and gradually add pasta so that the water keeps boiling briskly. Do not break the spaghetti, but place it in the water and as it softens, it will sink into the pot. Stir occasionally with a wooden spoon. Cook about 12 minutes or until pasta is cooked but firm. Drain in collander.

Fettuccini with Zucchini

Noodles tossed with a delicate blend of zucchini, shallots, tomatoes and cheese is practically a meal in itself.

2 tablespoons butter
2 tablespoons olive oil
1 onion
3 cloves garlic
2 shallots, minced
1 pound Italian zucchini, grated. Sprinkle with ½ teaspoon salt and allow to drain in a strainer. Press dry.

1 can (1 pound) stewed tomatoes, drained and finely chopped. Reserve juice for another use.

1 cup grated Gruyere or Swiss cheese
½ cup grated Parmesan cheese (or more to taste)

salt and freshly ground pepper to taste

1 package (½ pound) medium egg noodles cooked firm according to directions on the package. Toss hot, cooked noodles in 4 tablespoons melted butter.

Saute onion, garlic and shallots in butter and olive oil until the onion is transparent. Now add the zucchini and continue sauteing until the zucchini are tender. (If you prefer not to drain the zucchini, then you must saute them over moderately high heat, and cook them until the liquid evaporates. This takes about an extra 15 minutes.)

Add the chopped tomatoes and simmer mixture for 10 minutes. Sauce should be very thick and not soupy. Add salt and pepper.

Toss cooked noodles with zucchini tomato mixture and place in a pretty porcelain casserole. Sprinkle cheese over the top and heat in a 350° oven until heated through. Broil for a few seconds to brown top. Serves 6 as a main course or 8 as a side dish.

Note – Entire casserole can be assembled earlier in the day and refrigerated. Bring to room temperature before heating. Heat in a 350° oven for 20 minutes or until piping hot. Broil as described above.

Tartufo alla Tre Scalini Caffe

This delightful chocolate iced cream dessert is the famous specialty of the Caffe Tre Scalini in Rome. The original recipe is a zealously guarded secret, but using a very excellent quality chocolate ice cream is a good substitute and a lot easier on you.

16 glaceed cherries
2 tablespoons rum

8 large scoops of chocolate ice cream

1 package (12 ounces) semi-sweet chocolate chips
½ cup butter (1 stick)

1 cup toasted slivered almonds

Soak cherries in rum. With a large ice cream scooper, scoop out 8 balls of ice cream on a wax paper-lined cookie sheet. Press 2 cherries into each center, working quickly, and place in freezer until very firm.

In the top of a double boiler, over hot not boiling water, melt chocolate and butter together. Allow to cool. Spear each ice cream ball with a fork and quickly dip and roll it into the melted chocolate. Return it to the wax paper and sprinkle each ball with toasted walnuts. Work quickly and return these to the freezer until firm. Decorate with an additional rum-soaked cherry when serving. Serve in a lovely stemmed glass or glass dessert dish so that the lovely chocolate and nuts show through. Serves 8.

Note – This dessert can be made in stages. You can prepare the ice cream balls on one day, and do the chocolate dipping the next day. However, cover the ice cream with plastic wrap if you do this.
– Entire dessert can be prepared 2 or 3 days earlier and stored in the freezer well covered with plastic wrap.
– Remove from the freezer 5 minutes before serving.

A Roman Holiday

The Menu
Clams Florentine

Antipasto
Caponata, Marinated Mushrooms, Marinated Artichoke Hearts,
Smoked Oysters or Clams,
Imported Provelone Cheese, Biscotti Crackers

Panettone with Sweet Butter
or
Italian Bread with Lemon Herb Butter

Braccioli alla Marinara
Tortellini with Marinara Sauce
Herbed Zucchini Mold

Lemon Gelati and Espresso
or
Cassata Romano with Cappuccino

If you are planning a special dinner to celebrate a joyous event, or if you feel like going overboard at holiday time, I hope you will enjoy some of my favorite things in this Roman Holiday Menu. While it appears lengthy, follow these shortcuts carefully and you will have plenty of time to relax on the day of your dinner party.

To begin with, serve the Clams Florentine in your living room or den. Served in scallop shells, they are especially festive and offer an introduction of the good things to come. The antipasto will be set on your dining room table on a beautiful platter or lazy Susan and all of the items will be purchased in cans or jars. Simply arrange the tray attractively with lots of parsley or green leaves. The Tortellini are purchased frozen in an Italian market. You will need 1½ pounds for 12 servings.

If you choose not to make the bread, then purchase Italian Rolls or a long loaf and serve it with Lemon Herb Butter. If your company would prefer a light refreshing dessert, serve the Lemon Iced Cream and Espresso. If your guests like a dessert with more body, the Cassata Romano should delight even the most fastidious. It is truly one of my favorites.

Now, prepare a week earlier the Lemon Gelati, Cappucino and Liqueur Mixes. Prepare one day earlier the Clams Florentine, Marinara Sauce, Herbed Zucchini Mold, Cassata Romano and if you are careful in reheating, you can easily prepare the Braccioli also. On the day of your party, you only have to prepare the Tortellini and reheat the other dishes. Buon Gusto.

Herbed Clams Florentine with Mushrooms, Sour Cream and Cheese

Lovely, exciting and very delicious are these scallop shells filled with spinach, mushrooms, sour cream and herbs. The delicate sprinkling of cheese crumbs on top adds a delightful touch that I hope you enjoy.

2 packages frozen spinach (10 ounces, each) defrosted and drained and pressed dry

½ pound mushrooms, cleaned and sliced
1 onion, finely chopped
4 tablespoons butter

3 tablespoons flour
1 pint sour cream

salt and pepper to taste
pinch of thyme, sage and nutmeg (or use 3 pinches poultry seasoning)
2 cans (7 ounces, each) chopped clams, drained
3 tablespoons bread crumbs
2 tablespoons grated Parmesan cheese

Place spinach in a strainer and press to drain. Saute mushrooms and onion in butter until onions are soft. Add flour and cook for two minutes, stirring all the while. Add sour cream and seasonings. Stir to blend and heat through. Stir in the drained clams.

Divide mixture between 12 scallop shells. Combine crumbs and grated cheese. Sprinkle 1 teaspoon crumb mixture over each shell. Refrigerate until serving time.

Heat in a 350° oven before serving for about 30 minutes or until piping hot. Serves 12.

NOTE – Entire dish can be prepared and assembled one day earlier. Refrigerate until ready to heat before serving.

Panettone
(Italian Raisin Bread)

Bread and butter can be a gastronomical delight using this fragrant aromatic bread. It is very good with coffee and quite excellent with a glass of wine.

1/3 cup warm water (105^0 to 115^0)
3 packages active dry yeast
3 teaspoons sugar

3 eggs
¼ cup sugar
1 teaspoon vanilla
½ teaspoon salt

½ cup unsalted butter, melted and cooled
3 cups flour, lightly packed

½ cup yellow raisins
½ cup dark raisins

In a glass measuring cup, stir together warm water, yeast and sugar. Allow to stand until doubled in volume. This is called "proofing the yeast" and if it does not foam, yeast is not active and should be discarded.

In a large mixer bowl, beat eggs, sugar, vanilla and salt. Add yeast and beat until blended. Beat in melted butter and flour. If you have a dough hook, use it at this time. If not, then you must knead the dough until it is smooth and satiny, about 5 minutes. Shape into a ball and turn into a greased bowl. Cover and let rise in a warm place (85^0) until double in volume. Punch down dough and knead in the raisins. Shape into a ball and place into a 1½-quart souffle dish that is lightly greased and floured. Cover and let rise again until dough is doubled in volume.

With a knife, indent a cross on the top of the dough. Brush top with melted butter and bake in a 400^0 oven for 10 minutes. Reduce heat to 350^0 and continue baking for about 30 minutes or until top is a deep golden brown. A lovely crown will have formed and it will be studded with raisins. Allow to cool in baking dish on a rack. Slice with a serrated knife and serve 12 with grand ceremony.

Note: – Read this very detailed recipe carefully before you start. This is a beautiful bread and well worth the little extra work. Good luck!

Braccioli alla Marinara

(Roulades of Beef with Herb Stuffing, Bacon and Pine Nuts)

Incredibly easy and very delicious are these tender, succulent beef rolls, stuffed with an easy to prepare stuffing that is sparkled with bacon and pine nuts.

24 slices spencer steaks. Ask your butcher to slice these from the small end and ¼-inch thick.

1 package Stove Top Stuffing Mix, Chicken flavor, (6 ounces)
1 egg, beaten
½ cup toasted pine nuts
3 strips bacon, cooked crisp and crumbled

½ cup (1 stick) butter, about
¼ cup Cognac or brandy

Prepare stuffing mix according to the directions on the package, substituting canned beef broth (diluted) for the water. Stir in the beaten egg, pine nuts and bacon.

Place 1 tablespoon stuffing on end of each steak, roll up and fasten with a toothpick. Roll these in Seasoned Flour and saute the rolls in butter until meat loses its pinkness. Do not overcrowd the pan and do not overcook. Steaks are exceedingly tender. Warm Cognac in a brandy warmer, ignite and pour over beef rolls. (These can be made earlier in the day and refrigerated. Bring to room temperature and reheat in a 275° oven until heated through.) Serve hot and pass the sauce. Serves 12.

Seasoned Flour:
1 cup flour
2 teaspoons garlic powder
2 teaspoons paprika
1 teaspoon salt

Combine the ingredients in a plastic bag and shake until blended.

Salsa Marinara

1 can (1 pound 12 ounces) tomato puree
1 can (1 pound) stewed tomatoes, finely chopped
2 tablespoons chopped onion flakes (dry)
2 tablespoons sugar
2 tablespoons parsley flakes (dry)
2 tablespoons olive oil
¼ teaspoon garlic powder
salt and freshly ground pepper to taste

Combine all the ingredients and simmer for 10 minutes.

Herbed Zucchini Mold with Cheese, Onions and Garlic

1 pound zucchini, sliced. Not necessary to peel.
1 large onion, chopped
2 cloves garlic, put through a press
4 tablespoons butter

3 cups cottage cheese
1 cup grated Parmesan cheese
¾ cup breadcrumbs
½ teaspoon Italian Herb Seasoning

6 eggs, beaten
salt and pepper to taste

Saute zucchini, onion and garlic in butter until the onions are tender.

In a large bowl, mix together the zucchini mixture, cottage cheese, breadcrumbs and seasonings. Mix in the eggs until mixture is blended.

Spray a 2-cup mold with Pam or other non-stick coating. Heavily butter mold and sprinkle lightly with flour. Sprinkle paprika into mold. Spoon zucchini and cheese mixture into mold and spread to even.

Bake in a 350° oven for 1 hour or until top is golden brown and eggs are set. Allow to cool in pan for about 10 minutes. Loosen sides and invert onto serving platter. Decorate with lots of parsley. Serves 12.

Note: – *Recipe can be halved if you are serving 6.*
– *If you are planning to prepare this dish earlier in the day, then invert mold onto a heat and serve platter. Reheat in a 350° oven for about 20 minutes or until heated through.*
– *This dish can be reheated in a microwave oven for 3 minutes on High.*
– *This can be baked in a 9x13-inch pan and cut into squares when serving.*

Lemon Gelati

(Lemon Iced Cream)

1 pint whipping cream
4 tablespoons lemon juice
½ lemon, finely grated. Remove any large pieces of membranes
1 cup sugar

In a bowl, place all the ingredients and stir until the sugar is dissolved, about 1 minute. Divide the mixture between 12 paper-lined muffin cups. Place in the freezer until firm. When frozen firm, store in double plastic bags.

Remove from the freezer about 5 minutes before serving. To serve, remove the paper liners and place iced cream in a lovely stemmed glass or pretty glass dessert dish. Spoon a dollup of whipped cream over the top (optional) and then a spoonful of Raspberry Sauce (a must.) Serves 12.

Raspberry Sauce:
1 package (10 ounces) frozen raspberries in syrup, thawed
1 tablespoon lemon juice

Simply stir ingredients together until blended.

Herbed Lemon Butter

1 cup butter (2 sticks) softened
2 tablespoons lemon juice
¼ teaspoon Italian Herb Seasoning
½ teaspoon parsley flakes (dry)
½ teaspoon chopped chive flakes (dry)

Beat butter until light. Add remaining ingredients and beat until blended. Yields 1 cup herbed butter.

Cassata Romana with Chocolate and Raspberries

One day, when you are thinking of how to please or make some very special friends happy, you might like to prepare this grand cake, which is one of my favorites.

6 egg whites, at room temperature
½ cup sugar

6 egg yolks, at room temperature
½ cup sugar

1½ cups finely grated walnuts
1 teaspoon baking powder
1 teaspoon vanilla

Preheat oven to 350°. Butter a 10x15-inch jelly roll pan. Line it with waxed paper extending 4-inches beyond the ends of the pan. Butter the waxed paper. Set aside. Wet a towel and squeeze it until it is damp-dry.

Beat whites until foamy. Gradually add ½ cup sugar and continue beating until whites are stiff and glossy. Beat yolks with ½ cup sugar until mixture is very thick. Beat in nuts, baking powder and vanilla. Fold in beaten egg whites. Pour batter into prepared pan and bake at 350° for about 25 minutes or until top is golden and a cake tester inserted in center comes out clean. Immediately cover cake with damp towel. Allow cake to cool and then refrigerate. Leave towel on cake. This can be done 2 days ahead.

The day before serving, turn cake out on 2 overlapping strips of waxed paper that have been sprinkled with sifted powdered sugar. Remove baking paper and trim edges of cake. Cut cake into thirds, yielding 3 strips measuring 14x3-inches. Fill and frost with Chocolate Chip Whipped Cream and Raspberries. Sprinkle extra chocolate bits over the top and decorate with whole raspberries. Refrigerate overnight. Serves 12 very special friends.

Chocolate Chip Whipped Cream and Raspberries

1 pint whipping cream
2 tablespoons sugar
2 tablespoons Grand Marnier Liqueur
1 cup semi-sweet chocolate chips, coarsely chopped in blender or processor
1 package (10 ounces) frozen raspberries, drained

Beat cream with sugar and liqueur until stiff. Beat in chopped chocolate bits. Stir in drained raspberries. Will fill and frost above cake.

Cappuccino Supreme

Traditionally, Cappuccino is made with equal amounts of espresso coffee and hot milk. Served with a dollup of whipped cream and a sprinkling of cinnamon or nutmeg, it is very good indeed. However, the addition of liqueurs and cream adds a good deal of excitement and "spirit" to the occasion.

Cappuccino Mix

4 tablespoons instant espresso coffee
2 tablespoons cocoa
2 tablespoons sugar

Liqueurs

5 ounces coffee liqueur
5 ounces Creme de Cacao liqueur
2 ounces Cognac or brandy

4½ cups boiling water
1½ cups milk
1½ cups cream

Whipped cream
cinnamon, nutmeg or shaved chocolate

Combine instant coffee, cocoa and sugar in a jar with a tight fitting lid. In another jar, combine the liqueurs and brandy.

When you are ready to serve, boil the water and heat together the milk and cream.

Serving now is very simple. Place 1 teaspoon coffee mixture into each cup. Add about 3 ounces of boiling water, 2 ounces of hot milk mixture and 1 ounce of liqueur. Stir. Top with a dollup of whipped cream. Sprinkle lightly with cinnamon or nutmeg or shaved chocolate. Serves 12.

Note:
- *Cappuccino Mix can be stored for weeks and is very nice to have on hand. Use it as instant coffee.*
- *Liqueurs can be combined and stored indefinitely and are also nice to have ready when unexpected company arrives.*
- *If you are feeling adventuresome, try different combinations of your favorite liqueurs; Galliano (herb liqueur) or Amaretto (almond liqueur) or Frangelico (hazlenut liqueur) are especially good.*

Just Desserts

The Menu

Mocha Roulade with Chocolate Kahlua Cream

Chocolate Decadence
(Chocolate Rum Cake with Chocolate Mousse Frosting)

Pecan Torte with Raspberries, Whipped Cream
and Chocolate Curls

Sour Cream Apple Tart with Raisins

Pecan Butter Balls
Date Nut Bar Cookies
Apricot Walnut Chewies

Fresh Fruit Platter with Dessert Cheeses

Coffee and Tea

"Come for dessert." is a delightful way to entertain a large group for some special occasion like graduation or a family reunion or a get-together to celebrate a homecoming. You can accomodate a large number of guests without any last minute flutters.

Once you set up the dessert table and the area for coffee and tea, things very much seem to run themselves. Occasionally, you could check on the state of the cream and sugar, but, for the most part, you can delight in the fun with total abandon.

All of these grand desserts can be made two days ahead and frosted the day before your party. Pick as many as you need for the number of guests you are inviting. Be certain to have enough platters of the right size and separate serving pieces for each cake.

Fresh fruit with dessert cheeses should be set on an extravagant platter and decorated luxuriously with an abundance of leaves. Some excellent choices of cheese would be Gourmandise (cherry cheese), Danish Cream with Peaches, Rambol (with walnuts, pistachios or almonds) or a Light Brie (Tomme de Nieges–[wheel of snow]) would be just lovely. Use a very bland soda cracker so as to not interfere with the wonderful tastes of the cheese.

Mocha Roulade with Chocolate Kahlua Cream

6 egg whites
½ cup sugar

6 egg yolks
½ cup sugar

2 cups very finely grated walnuts
1 teaspoon baking powder

Preheat oven to 350°. Butter a 10x15-inch jelly roll pan. Line it with waxed paper extending 4-inches beyond the ends of the pan. Butter the waxed paper. Set aside. Wet a towel and squeeze until it is damp-dry.

In a large mixing bowl, beat egg whites until foamy. Continue beating and adding ½ cup sugar slowly, until whites are still and glossy.

Beat yolks with ½ cup sugar slowly until mixture is very thick. Beat in grated nuts and baking powder only until blended. Fold in beaten egg whites. Pour batter into prepared pan and spread evenly. Bake at 350° for about 25 minutes or until top of cake is golden and a cake tester inserted in cake comes out clean. Immediately cover cake with slightly dampened towel. Allow cake to cool and then refrigerate. Leave towel on cake. This can be done 2 days ahead.

The day before serving, turn cake out on 2 overlapping strips of waxed paper. Remove baking paper and trim edges of cake. Spread Chocolate Kahlua Cream over cake. Using the waxed paper to help you, roll cake up and place on long serving platter. Frost with remaining cream. Drizzle several teaspoons of chocolate syrup over the cake, to decorate. Serves 12 very fortunate friends.

Chocolate Kahlua Cream

2 cups cream
2 teaspoons instant coffee powder
¾ cup chocolate syrup
2 tablespoons Kahlua Liqueur

Beat cream with coffee powder until blended. Gradually add chocolate syrup and liqueur and continue beating until cream is stiff.

Chocolate Decadence

(Chocolate Rum Cake with Chocolate Mousse Frosting)

4 eggs
1 cup sugar
1 tablespoon rum
1 teaspoon vanilla

4 tablespoons cocoa, sifted
½ cup almond meal (purchased at health food stores)
4 tablespoons bread crumbs
½ cup butter, melted

Beat eggs with sugar, rum and vanilla until mixture is very light and tripled in volume, about 5 minutes at highest speed.

Combine cocoa, almond meal and bread crumbs and fold into egg mixture. Slowly fold in melted butter. Pour batter into a buttered 9-inch spring-form pan and bake in a 350° oven for about 25 minutes or until a cake tester inserted in center comes out clean.

Cool cake in pan and remove ring. Place cake on a beautiful footed platter. Pour Chocolate Mousse Frosting over the top and let it drizzle down the sides. Refrigerate cake overnight. Remove cake from refrigerator about 15 minutes before serving. Serves 8 to 10.

Chocolate Mousse Frosting

1 package (6 ounces) semi-sweet chocolate chips
¾ cup cream
2 egg yolks
1 tablespoon rum

Place chocolate chips in blender container. Heat cream to boiling point and pour into blender. Blend for 1 minute. Chocolate will have melted. Add yolks and rum and continue blending 1 minute more. Allow frosting to cool and thicken slightly before spreading on cake.

NOTE – If you really want to go overboard, sprinkle some shaved chocolate over the top. To shave chocolate, run a vegetable peeler down the side of a refrigerated chocolate bar.

Pecan Torte with Raspberries, Whipped Cream and Chocolate Curls

This recipe makes 1 layer.

4 eggs
1 cup shelled pecans

¾ cup sugar
1 teaspoon vanilla
2 tablespoons flour
2 teaspoons baking powder

½ cup seedless red raspberry jam
1 basket (½ pint) red raspberries

Place eggs in blender container and whip at high speed for a few seconds. Add pecans and blend for another few seconds. Add sugar, vanilla, flour and baking powder and blend for 1 minute more. Pour batter into a 10-inch layer pan with a removable bottom, that has been lightly buttered and floured. Repeat for second layer.

Bake 2 layers at the same time in a 350° oven for about 20-25 minutes or until a cake tester inserted in center comes out clean.

Remove from oven and cool layers in pan. Remove metal rings. When cool, remove layer (use a sharp knife) and place on your prettiest footed cake plate. Melt the raspberry jam and add the raspberries. Stir to coat raspberries. Place raspberry mixture over the first layer. Top this with ⅓ the whipped cream. Place second layer over the whipped cream. Frost top and sides with remaining whipped cream. Decorate top with chocolate curls. Serves 10 to 12.

Whipped Cream Chantilly

1 pint whipping cream
2 tablespoons sugar
1 teaspoon vanilla

Beat cream with sugar and vanilla until stiff.

NOTE – This exquisite torte can be made and frosted the day before serving.
– Chocolate curls can be made by running a vegetable peeler down the sides of a chocolate bar that is at room temperature.

Sour Cream Apple Tart with Raisins

Fresh apples on a vanilla walnut crust painted with apricot and topped with sour cream. What a wonderful union of flavors and textures that will surely delight family and friends.

2 cups yellow cake mix
6 tablespoons butter
½ cup chopped walnuts

4 tablespoons apricot jam
2 apples, peeled and grated
¼ cup yellow raisins

1 cup sour cream
1 egg
3 tablespoons sugar

In your electric mixer, beat cake mix and butter until the mixture is blended. Add the walnuts and mix well. With your fingers, pat dough evenly on the bottom and sides of an ungreased 10-inch tart pan with a removable bottom. Bake crust in a preheated 350° oven for 8 minutes.

Spread apricot jam evenly over the crust (carefully, so that you do not burn your fingers). Place apples evenly over the jam and sprinkle top with raisins. Beat together the sour cream, egg and sugar until blended. Pour mixture over the apples. Return to oven and continue baking at 350° for about 35 minutes or until top is lightly browned. Serves 8.

NOTE – Apple tart can be made earlier in the day and refrigerated.
– While it is delicious served warm, it is also very good served at room temperature.

Pecan Butter Balls

1 cup butter, (2 sticks)
½ cup sifted powdered sugar
1½ cups finely chopped pecans
2 cups cake flour
2 teaspoons vanilla

Cream butter with sugar. Add remaining ingredients and mix until blended. Shape dough into ¾-inch balls. Place balls on a lightly buttered cookie sheet and bake in a 300° oven for about 25 to 30 minutes.

Roll cookies in sifted powdered sugar when warm and again when cold. Yields about 60 cookies.

Date Nut Bar Cookies

½ cup butter (1 stick)
⅓ cup sugar
1 cup flour

2 eggs
1 cup brown sugar
⅓ cup flour
½ teaspoon baking powder
1 teaspoon vanilla
½ cup chopped nuts
¾ cup chopped dates

Beat together butter, sugar and flour until mixture resembles coarse meal. Lightly butter an 8x8-inch pan and pat dough evenly over the bottom. Bake at 350° for about 20 minutes or until dough is lightly browned.

Meanwhile beat together the eggs, sugar, flour, baking powder and vanilla until blended. Stir in nuts and dates. Pour egg mixture evenly over baked dough. Bake an additional 25 minutes or until topping is set. Cool in pan and cut into bars. Dust lightly with sifted powdered sugar. Yields about 36 cookies.

Apricot Walnut Chewies

2 cups yellow cake mix
½ cup butter (1 stick)

1 jar (12 ounces) fruity apricot jam
1½ cups coarsely chopped walnuts
½ cup coconut flakes

1 can (14 ounces) condensed milk

Beat together cake mix and butter until blended. Pat mixture on the bottom of a 9x13-inch pan. You can do this with your fingers or a spatula. Spread apricot jam evenly over the dough. Sprinkle nuts and coconut over the jam. Drizzle condensed milk evenly over all.

Bake cookies in a 350° oven for about 30 or 35 minutes or until topping is golden brown. Allow to cool in pan. Cut into squares and sprinkle lightly with sifted powdered sugar. Yields about 48 chewies.

Easy Date Nut Bar Cookies

½ cup (1 stick) butter
2 cups yellow cake mix
2 cups chopped dates
4 tablespoons cinnamon sugar
1 cup chopped walnuts

1 can (14 ounces) condensed milk

In a 9x13-inch pan, melt the butter and spread it evenly over the bottom. Now, layer and sprinkle evenly over the butter, the cake mix, dates, cinnamon sugar and walnuts. Drizzle the condensed milk evenly over all.

Bake in a 350° oven for about 30 to 35 minutes or until the top is golden brown. Allow to cool in pan. Cut into 1½-inch squares and serve with a faint sprinkling of sifted powdered sugar. Yields 48 delectable cookies.

Great Beginnings and Endings

The following are a few of my favorite things that I thought you might enjoy.

Mushrooms Stuffed with Crabmeat, Cheese and Chives

1 pound mushrooms, clean and remove stems. Brush mushrooms, inside and out, with melted butter.

½ pound crabmeat, pick over for bones
3 packages, (3 ounces, each) cream cheese with chives
½ cup grated Swiss cheese
⅓ cup garlic croutons, crushed into fine crumbs

grated Parmesan cheese
paprika

Beat together the crabmeat, cream cheese, Swiss cheese and croutons until the mixture is blended. Mound mixture in mushroom caps. Sprinkle tops generously with grated Parmesan cheese and paprika.

Place caps on a cookie sheet and bake in a 350° oven until piping hot. Place under the broiler for a few seconds to brown. Serve at once.

Note – Mushrooms can be assembled earlier in the day and refrigerated. Heat through before serving.

Cocktail Frankfurters in Sweet and Sour Currant Sauce

1 pound cocktail-size frankfurters

½ cup chili sauce
1 cup currant jelly
4 tablespoons brown sugar
2 tablespoons lemon juice

Heat together the chili sauce, currant jelly, brown sugar and lemon juice and simmer for 2 minutes. Add the franks and simmer for another 5 minutes. Place the mixture in a chafing dish. Serve with picks or spears.

Crown Mold of Crabmeat Mousse Royale

1 package (1 tablespoon) unflavored gelatin
¼ cup cold water

⅔ cup mayonnaise, at room temperature
4 tablespoon lemon juice
1 green onion, finely chopped
2 tablespoons finely chopped parsley
2 tablespoons finely chopped chives
2 teaspoons Dijon-style mustard
salt and pepper to taste

½ cup sour cream
½ pound cooked crabmeat

Soften gelatin in cold water and place it over hot water until dissolved. Add mayonnaise, lemon juice, onion, parsley, chives, mustard and seasonings and stir until blended. Fold in sour cream and crabmeat.

Pour mixture into a 4-cup ring mold and refrigerate until firm. Unmold onto a lovely footed platter and decorate with green onion frills, lemon slices sprinkled with parsley and cherry tomatoes.

An Elegant Puff Pastry Cheese and Chive Pie

1 package frozen patty shells (6) slightly defrosted

¼ cup grated Parmesan cheese
1 cup grated Swiss cheese
¼ cup chopped chives
¼ teaspoon paprika
pinch of salt and pepper

Stack 3 patty shells together and roll out to measure 8-inches. Combine cheeses, chives and seasonings and place in center of dough. Roll remaining shells in the same fashion and place over the cheese. Press and seal the edges and scallop them in a decorative fashion. Pierce top with the times of a fork, brush with a little water and sprinkle with additional grated Parmesan cheese. Can be held at this point for several hours in the refrigerator.

Bake in a 400° oven for about 20 to 25 minutes or until top is a deep golden brown. Serve on a lovely platter and cut into wedges. Serves 6.

Sesame Chicken Wings with Honey Barbecue Glaze

This is perhaps one of the easiest barbecue sauces that I have ever used. I am always amazed at how anything this simple could be so good.

3 pounds of chicken wings, remove wing tips, sprinkle with salt, garlic powder and teriyaki marinade. (Use the prepared marinade for this recipe.)
Sesame seeds

Place chicken in a 9x13-inch roasting pan. Bake in a 350° oven for 20 minutes. Now, start basting with Honey Barbecue Glaze and continue baking for 25 minutes. Chicken will be a rich golden brown. Sprinkle with sesame seeds and bake for an additional 10 minutes.

Honey Barbecue Glaze

1 cup barbecue sauce (use a good quality sauce)
1 cup honey

Cook together the barbecue sauce and honey until the mixture is well blended. Store any unused sauce in the refrigerator.

Note – Don't reserve this simple dish for a party. It is also very good for dinner.

Chicken Wings Teriyaki

3 pounds of chicken wings, sprinkle with salt and garlic powder.

Place chicken wings in a 9x13-inch roasting pan. Pour Teriyaki marinade over the chicken and bake in a 350° oven for about 45 minutes, turning and basting frequently. Tent lightly if chicken browns too rapidly.

Teriyaki Marinade

1 cup soy sauce
1 cup brown sugar
¼ cup butter (½ stick)

Cook together all the ingredients until the sugar is melted.

Piroshki with Onions and Beef

The Pastry:
1 cup butter (2 sticks)
½ pound cream cheese
2 cups flour
pinch of salt

In the large bowl of an electric mixer, cream together butter and cream cheese until blended. Add flour and salt and mix at low speed until the flour is incorporated and even. Place dough on floured waxed paper and sprinkle top with additional flour to make for easier handling. Shape into an 8-inch circle and wrap it in the waxed paper and then foil. Refrigerate overnight.

Divide dough into four parts. Working one part at a time, roll it out on a floured pastry cloth until the dough is approximately ⅛-inch thick. Cut with a cookie or biscuit cutter into 2¾-inch round and accumulate scraps in the refrigerator to roll out at the end.

Place ½ teaspoon Beef Onion Filling on center of each round, moisten the edges and fold over. Press edges down with the tines of a fork. Sprinkle top with grated Parmesan cheese.

Place piroshkis on a buttered cookie sheet and bake at 350° for about 25 minutes or until tops are lightly browned. Yields about 50 piroshki.

Beef Onion Filling:
¾ pound lean ground beef
2 tablespoons dried onion flakes
2 tablespoons flour
1 cup sour cream
¼ teaspoon thyme
salt, pepper and garlic powder to taste

Saute meat with onion flakes until meat loses its pinkness. Add flour and stir for 2 minutes. Add sour cream and seasonings and continue cooking and stirring until mixture is thickened, about 2 minutes. Allow to cool.

Note – Piroshkis can be frozen unbaked or baked.

Petite Souffles with Mushrooms and Swiss Cheese

This very lovely souffle is an excellent small entree, a delightful hors d'hoeurve and a wonderful choice for a luncheon dish. Mushrooms, sauteed in butter with shallots, and sparkled with herbs and cream is a grand combination with the delicate Swiss cheese.

½ pound mushrooms, thinly sliced
2 tablespoons shallots, finely chopped
4 tablespoons butter

2 tablespoons flour
¾ cup cream
salt and pepper to taste
⅛ teaspoon poultry seasoning

6 eggs
½ pound cream cheese
1 cup grated Swiss cheese
salt and pepper to taste

Saute mushrooms and shallots in butter over moderately high heat until mushrooms are tender and liquid is absorbed. Add flour and cook for 2 minutes, stirring. Add the cream and seasonings and continue to cook and stir until sauce is thickened, about 2 minutes.

Beat eggs with cream cheese until mixture is thoroughly blended. Beat in the Swiss cheese and seasonings. Combine mushroom and egg mixtures and stir until blended.

Divide mixture evenly between 6 lightly buttered ramekins and bake in a 375° oven for about 20 minutes or until eggs are set and top is lightly browned. Serve immediately. Serves 6.

Note – Souffle can be assembled several hours earlier and stored in the refrigerator until baking time.
– Sprinkling tops with a teaspoon of grated Parmesan cheese is a nice optional.
– You may prefer to bake souffle in a 9x11-inch bake and serve porcelain casserole. In that case, bake for about 30 minutes or until eggs are set and top is a golden brown.

Clams with Garlic and Herb Stuffing

3 cans minced clams (7 ounces each) drained. Reserve juice.
1 package prepared herbed stuffing
¼ pound butter, melted
2 cloves garlic, minced
1 teaspoon Italian Herb Seasoning
1 tablespoon chopped parsley
3 tablespoons finely minced onion
6 tablespoons grated Parmesan cheese
salt and pepper to taste

Combine all the ingredients and toss until well mixed. Now, slowly add the reserved clam broth until the stuffing holds together and is moist. Do not let filling get soggy or stay too dry. Divide mixture between 12 clam shells. Sprinkle with paprika and a pinch of oregano.

Place clam shells on a cookie sheet and heat in a 350° oven until piping hot. Brown under the broiler for a few seconds until golden. Serves 12 as a first course.

Petite Muffins for Hors d'oeuvres

2 eggs
1 cup small curd cottage cheese
2 tablespoons sour cream
1 tablespoon oil
1 teaspoon sugar
½ cup grated Parmesan cheese
½ cup Bisquick

Beat eggs. Add remaining ingredients and beat together until blended. Grease hors d'oeuvre-size teflon-lined muffin pans. Fill ½ full with batter. Bake in a preheated 350° oven for 25 minutes or until puffed and lightly browned. Yields 24-30 muffins.

Note – *Serve these warm with a dollup of sour cream and caviar or with sour cream and a thin slice of smoked salmon. You may enjoy them with cream cheese whipped with shrimp or crabmeat which is also very good. They are delicious "natural" as well.*

Fresh Vegetable Platter with Sauce Verte

Arrange a large platter of sliced carrots, celery, cucumbers, zucchini, mushrooms, cherry tomatoes, jicama, etc. in any combination you desire. Slice the vegetables straight, on the diagonal, into circles, sticks, curls, etc. Arrange on a bed of lettuce. Dip the ends of the lettuce leaves in paprika for a pretty effect. Place the Imperial Sauce Verte in the center and Voila! you have a party.

Many friends have said that my Sauce Verte is the best they have ever tasted. I hope you enjoy it too.

Imperial Sauce Verte

½ cup frozen spinach, defrosted and drained

3 sprigs parsley, stems removed, use only the leaves
2 green onions, use the green tops and the white bulbs
1 cup mayonnaise
½ cup sour cream
1½ tablespoons lemon juice
salt to taste

Place spinach in strainer and drain liquid. Set aside. Place remaining ingredients in blender and blend at high speed until smooth. Combine spinach and blended ingredients and mix well. Refrigerate until ready to use. Makes 2 cups.

Herbed Tomato Onion Salad with Garlic and Lemon

6 tomatoes, thinly sliced
1 medium onion, sliced into rings as thin as possible
1 teaspoon basil
4 tablespoons olive oil
3 tablespoons lemon juice
1 clove garlic, put through a press
salt and freshly ground pepper to taste

Combine tomatoes, onion and basil in a bowl. In a jar, combine oil, lemon, garlic and seasonings and shake to blend. Pour dressing over tomatoes and toss to coat well. Refrigerate salad for several hours to allow flavors to blend. Serves 6.

Potage of Tomatoes and Clams

1 can (1 pound) stewed tomatoes, finely chopped
1 can (8 ounces) tomato sauce
1 cup tomato juice
1 cup clam juice
2 tablespoons oil
1 teaspoon sugar
1 onion, finely chopped
1 clove garlic, mashed
½ teaspoon thyme flakes
pinch of tumeric
2 tablespoons chopped parsley
salt and pepper to taste

Combine all the ingredients in a large saucepan and simmer mixture for 30 minutes. Add

2 cups half and half
2 cans (7 ounces, each) chopped clams

and heat through. Serve with some crusty French bread and sweet butter. Serves 6.

Note – Soup base can be made one or two days earlier. Reheat soup, add the cream and the clams and continue heating until soup is piping hot.
– If you like, float 1 teaspoon of sour cream on soup when serving.
– A wonderful touch would be to serve the soup with Croustades of French Bread with Cheese.

Croustades of French Bread with Cheese

6 slices French bread, lightly toasted

4 tablespoons mayonnaise
6 tablespoons grated Swiss cheese
1 clove garlic, put through a press
1 tablespoon lemon juice

Combine mayonnaise, cheese, garlic and lemon juice. Spread mixture evenly between the 6 slices of bread. When ready to serve, broil bread for a few seconds or until top is lightly browned and bubbly.

Note – Bread can be assembled earlier in the day and placed in pan. Cover well with plastic wrap. Remove plastic before broiling.

2-Minute Souffle au Grand Marnier with Chestnut Cream

One day, when you have nothing better to do, and are looking for a standing ovation or to be swept off your feet, or seriously looking for a grand finale for dinner, you would do well to consider this totally indescribable majestic dessert. When you consider that it takes 2-minutes to assemble and it can also be assembled in advance, you will keep this little treasure handy when you are looking for a little "social security."

5 eggs
1 package (8 ounces) cream cheese, cut into 4 pieces
¾ cup cream
¼ cup Grand Marnier Liqueur
½ cup sugar

Place all the ingredients in a food processor or blender container. Blend for 2 minutes. Pour the mixture into a 1½-quart souffle dish that has been buttered and dusted lightly with sugar.

Bake in a 375° oven for about 50 minutes or until top is crowned and golden brown. Serve immediately with a spoonful of Chestnut Cream or lightly whipped cream. Serves 6.

Note – *Not the least of its glorious virtues is that this souffle can be assembled several hours earlier and stored in the refrigerator. Remove from the refrigerator about 10 minutes before baking. Bake as described above.*
– *Serve at once or souffle will fall.*

Chestnut Whipped Cream

1 cup cream, whipped
¼ cup sweetened chestnut puree (purchased in a can)
1 tablespoon Cognac

Whip cream until stiff. Beat in the chestnut puree and Cognac.

Note – *If you do not have the time to whip the cream, serve the souffle with a teaspoonful of defrosted raspberries in syrup. Don't feel for a moment that this isn't a lovely optional . . . stuck as it is on the bottom of the page.*

Chocolate Chip Pecan Pie with Creme de Chocolat

Crunchy chocolate chips and pecans are combined in this "easy as pie" dessert. This is my daughter's favorite and one of my favorites also.

3 eggs
½ cup sugar

2 cups vanilla wafer crumbs
½ cup sugar
1 teaspoon baking powder
1 teaspoon vanilla

1 cup coarsely chopped pecans
1 cup semi-sweet chocolate chips

Beat eggs with ½ cup sugar until light and fluffy, about 5 minutes at high speed. Stir in the remaining ingredients until blended.

Pour batter into a 9-inch lightly buttered pie plate and bake at 350° for 30 minutes. Frost with Creme de Chocolat and refrigerate for 6 hours or overnight. Serves 6.

Creme de Chocolat

1 cup cream
1 tablespoon sugar
1 tablespoon Cacao liqueur
¼ cup crushed semi-sweet chocolate chips

Beat cream with sugar and liqueur until stiff. Beat in chocolate chips.

Note – Pie can be frozen with or without frosting. Wrap in double thicknesses of plastic wrap and then foil. Allow to thaw in the refrigerator if frozen with the frosting.

Brownie Cake with Chocolate Buttercream

This very simple cake is extremely moist and chocolaty. You will enjoy the fact that it assembles easily, can be frozen and is very much like a delicate genoise.

2 cups flour
2 cups sugar
1 teaspoon baking soda

½ cup butter (1 stick)
1 cup water
¼ cup unsweetened cocoa

½ cup sour cream
2 eggs
2 teaspoons vanilla
1 cup chopped walnuts

Place flour, sugar and baking soda in large bowl of mixer. In a saucepan, heat together butter, water and cocoa to boiling point. Pour butter mixture into bowl with flour mixture and beat for 1 minute or until blended. Beat in sour cream, eggs and vanilla until blended. Stir in nuts.

Pour batter into a 10½x15½-inch jelly roll pan that has been lightly greased and floured. (If you use a teflon pan, you need not grease or flour pan.) Bake in a 350° oven for 20 minutes or until a cake tester inserted in center comes out clean. Do not overbake. Frost with Chocolate Buttercream Frosting when cool. Cut into squares and serve at room temperature. Yields about 15 servings, 3-inches each.

Note – If you prepare the cake a day earlier, store it in the refrigerator. Allow to come to room temperature before serving.

Chocolate Buttercream Frosting

½ cup butter (1 stick), melted
¼ cup unsweetened cocoa
⅓ cup sour cream
2½ cups sifted powdered sugar
1 teaspoon vanilla

Combine melted butter and cocoa. Stir in sour cream. Beat in powdered sugar and vanilla until of spreading consistency.

A Glorious Chocolate Mousse Cake

Chocolate lovers rejoice. This very simple (but by no means plain) and elegant mousse cake has a texture somewhat like a cheesecake and is so rich and chocolaty it will please the most refined chocolate palate.

½ cup (1 stick) butter
½ pound semi-sweet chocolate chips
2 tablespoons flour
1 tablespoon Grand Marnier Liqueur
1 teaspoon vanilla

5 eggs
¾ cup sugar

In the top of a double boiler over hot water, melt the butter. Add the chocolate chips and stir until chocolate is melted and mixture is smooth. Stir in flour, liqueur and vanilla. Allow to cool for about 10 minutes.

Meanwhile, beat the eggs and sugar together at high speed until the eggs are very light and fluffy about 6 minutes. With the beaters turning at low speed, fold in the melted chocolate mixture until blended.

Pour into an 8-inch buttered and floured springform pan and bake in a 250° oven for 1 hour.

Allow to cool in pan. Refrigerate for 4 to 6 hours. Overnight is better. Remove springform ring but leave cake on metal bottom. Place on your loveliest platter and decorate top with a delicate sprinkle of powdered sugar. Keep the portions small. Serves 10.

Note – Cake will rise then sink to its original volume. The top will form the thinnest crisp crust. This is normal.
– Cake should be served cold.
– This lovely mousse cake deserves a sprinkling of Vanilla sugar.

Vanilla Sugar

Place 1 pound of sifted powdered sugar into a cannister or jar with a tight fitting lid. Snap two vanilla beans sharply in thirds and bury them in the sugar. Use on pastries, cakes and wherever powdered sugar is called for. The beans will impart a gentle hint of vanilla to the sugar which is very delicate and very good indeed.

Old Fashioned Honey Spice Pumpkin Pie

Sometimes, it feels good to go back to basics. This is a traditional, old-fashioned pie with a touch of honey and spice and everything nice.

1 deep dish frozen pie shell (9-inch). Prebake in a 375° oven for 8 minutes. Brush bottom with 2 tablespoons apricot jam.

1 can (1 pound) pumpkin
¾ cup brown sugar
¼ teaspoon salt
2 teaspoons pumpkin pie spice
2 eggs, beaten
1½ cups half and half (can use cream if you're not counting)
¼ cup honey
1 tablespoon bourbon

Prepare pie shell. Combine the remaining ingredients and beat until blended. Pour mixture into prepared pie shell and place pie on a cookie sheet. (This will help crust to brown better and will facilitate removing the pie from the oven.) Bake in a 375° oven for about 50 minutes or until a knife inserted in center comes out clean. Cool. Serve with a dollup of whipped cream flavored with bourbon. Serves 6 to 8.

German Chocolate Pecan Pie

1 regular frozen pie shell (9-inch). Prebake in a 375° oven for 8 minutes.

1 cup chopped pecans
½ cup coconut flakes

¾ cup milk chocolate chips
¼ cup (½ stick) butter, softened
½ cup sugar
¾ cup cream, at room temperature
3 eggs, at room temperature
1 teaspoon vanilla

Prepare pie crust. Sprinkle pecans and coconut on bottom of crust. Heat together chocolate, butter and sugar until chocolate is melted. Cool slightly and beat in cream, eggs and vanilla until blended. Pour mixture into prepared pie crust and bake in a 375° oven for about 45 to 50 minutes or until a knife inserted in center comes out clean. Cool. Serves 6 to 8.

The Party Plans

Guest List	ACCEPTED	DECLINED	Guest List	ACCEPTED	DECLINED

Seating Arrangement

Comments

Occasion ______________ *Date* ______________

Theme ______________ *Time* ______________

MENU & BEVERAGES	LIST	SERVING PIECES	LIST	SHOPPING LIST

TABLE SETTING & DECORATIONS	LIST	MASTER LIST	LIST	
CHINA		INVITATIONS		
SILVER		FOOD		
CRYSTAL		BEVERAGES		
LINENS		WINES/LIQUORS		
CENTERPIECE/CANDLES		FLOWERS		
DECORATIONS		GAMES/ENTERTAINMENT		
OTHER		RENTAL/SERVICES		

Guest List	ACCEPTED	DECLINED	Guest List	ACCEPTED	DECLINED

Seating Arrangement

Comments

Occasion ______________________ *Date* ______________

Theme ______________________ *Time* ______________

MENU & BEVERAGES	LIST	SERVING PIECES	LIST	SHOPPING LIST

TABLE SETTING & DECORATIONS	LIST	MASTER LIST	LIST	
CHINA		INVITATIONS		
SILVER		FOOD		
CRYSTAL		BEVERAGES		
LINENS		WINES/LIQUORS		
CENTERPIECE/CANDLES		FLOWERS		
DECORATIONS		GAMES/ENTERTAINMENT		
OTHER		RENTAL/SERVICES		

Guest List	ACCEPTED	DECLINED	Guest List	ACCEPTED	DECLINED

Seating Arrangement

Comments

Occasion ______________ *Date* ______________

Theme ______________ *Time* ______________

MENU & BEVERAGES	LIST	SERVING PIECES	LIST	SHOPPING LIST

TABLE SETTING & DECORATIONS	LIST	MASTER LIST	LIST	
CHINA		INVITATIONS		
SILVER		FOOD		
CRYSTAL		BEVERAGES		
LINENS		WINES/LIQUORS		
CENTERPIECE/CANDLES		FLOWERS		
DECORATIONS		GAMES/ENTERTAINMENT		
OTHER		RENTAL/SERVICES		

Guest List	ACCEPTED	DECLINED	Guest List	ACCEPTED	DECLINED

Seating Arrangement

Comments

Occasion ______________________ *Date* ______________

Theme ______________________ *Time* ______________

MENU & BEVERAGES	LIST	SERVING PIECES	LIST	SHOPPING LIST

TABLE SETTING & DECORATIONS	LIST	MASTER LIST	LIST	
CHINA		INVITATIONS		
SILVER		FOOD		
CRYSTAL		BEVERAGES		
LINENS		WINES/LIQUORS		
CENTERPIECE/CANDLES		FLOWERS		
DECORATIONS		GAMES/ENTERTAINMENT		
OTHER		RENTAL/SERVICES		

Guest List	ACCEPTED	DECLINED	Guest List	ACCEPTED	DECLINED

Seating Arrangement

Comments

Occasion ____________________ *Date* ______________

Theme ____________________ *Time* ______________

MENU & BEVERAGES	LIST	SERVING PIECES	LIST	SHOPPING LIST

TABLE SETTING & DECORATIONS	LIST	MASTER LIST	LIST	
CHINA		INVITATIONS		
SILVER		FOOD		
CRYSTAL		BEVERAGES		
LINENS		WINES/LIQUORS		
CENTERPIECE/CANDLES		FLOWERS		
DECORATIONS		GAMES/ENTERTAINMENT		
OTHER		RENTAL/SERVICES		

Guest List	ACCEPTED	DECLINED	Guest List	ACCEPTED	DECLINED

Seating Arrangement

Comments

Occasion ______________________ *Date* ______________

Theme ______________________ *Time* ______________

MENU & BEVERAGES	✓ LIST	SERVING PIECES	✓ LIST	SHOPPING LIST

TABLE SETTING & DECORATIONS	✓ LIST	MASTER LIST	✓ LIST	
CHINA		INVITATIONS		
SILVER		FOOD		
CRYSTAL		BEVERAGES		
LINENS		WINES/LIQUORS		
CENTERPIECE/CANDLES		FLOWERS		
DECORATIONS		GAMES/ENTERTAINMENT		
OTHER		RENTAL/SERVICES		

Guest List	ACCEPTED	DECLINED	Guest List	ACCEPTED	DECLINED

Seating Arrangement

Comments

Occasion ______________________ *Date* ______________

Theme ________________________ *Time* ______________

MENU & BEVERAGES	LIST	SERVING PIECES	LIST	SHOPPING LIST

TABLE SETTING & DECORATIONS	LIST	MASTER LIST	LIST	
CHINA		INVITATIONS		
SILVER		FOOD		
CRYSTAL		BEVERAGES		
LINENS		WINES/LIQUORS		
CENTERPIECE/CANDLES		FLOWERS		
DECORATIONS		GAMES/ENTERTAINMENT		
OTHER		RENTAL/SERVICES		

Guest List	ACCEPTED	DECLINED	Guest List	ACCEPTED	DECLINED

Seating Arrangement

Comments

Occasion ______________________ *Date* ______________

Theme ______________________ *Time* ______________

MENU & BEVERAGES	LIST	SERVING PIECES	LIST	SHOPPING LIST

TABLE SETTING & DECORATIONS	LIST	MASTER LIST	LIST	
CHINA		INVITATIONS		
SILVER		FOOD		
CRYSTAL		BEVERAGES		
LINENS		WINES/LIQUORS		
CENTERPIECE/CANDLES		FLOWERS		
DECORATIONS		GAMES/ENTERTAINMENT		
OTHER		RENTAL/SERVICES		

Guest List	ACCEPTED	DECLINED	Guest List	ACCEPTED	DECLINED

Seating Arrangement

Comments

Occasion ______________________ *Date* ______________

Theme ______________________ *Time* ______________

MENU & BEVERAGES	LIST	SERVING PIECES	LIST	SHOPPING LIST

TABLE SETTING & DECORATIONS	LIST	MASTER LIST	LIST	
CHINA		INVITATIONS		
SILVER		FOOD		
CRYSTAL		BEVERAGES		
LINENS		WINES/LIQUORS		
CENTERPIECE/CANDLES		FLOWERS		
DECORATIONS		GAMES/ENTERTAINMENT		
OTHER		RENTAL/SERVICES		

Guest List	ACCEPTED	DECLINED	Guest List	ACCEPTED	DECLINED

Seating Arrangement

Comments

Occasion ______________________ *Date* ______________

Theme ______________________ *Time* ______________

MENU & BEVERAGES	✓ LIST	SERVING PIECES	✓ LIST	SHOPPING LIST

TABLE SETTING & DECORATIONS	✓ LIST	MASTER LIST	✓ LIST	
CHINA		INVITATIONS		
SILVER		FOOD		
CRYSTAL		BEVERAGES		
LINENS		WINES/LIQUORS		
CENTERPIECE/CANDLES		FLOWERS		
DECORATIONS		GAMES/ENTERTAINMENT		
OTHER		RENTAL/SERVICES		

Guest List	ACCEPTED	DECLINED	Guest List	ACCEPTED	DECLINED

Seating Arrangement

Comments

Occasion ____________________ *Date* ____________

Theme ______________________ *Time* ____________

MENU & BEVERAGES	LIST	SERVING PIECES	LIST	SHOPPING LIST

TABLE SETTING & DECORATIONS	LIST	MASTER LIST	LIST	
CHINA		INVITATIONS		
SILVER		FOOD		
CRYSTAL		BEVERAGES		
LINENS		WINES/LIQUORS		
CENTERPIECE/CANDLES		FLOWERS		
DECORATIONS		GAMES/ENTERTAINMENT		
OTHER		RENTAL/SERVICES		

Guest List	ACCEPTED	DECLINED

Guest List	ACCEPTED	DECLINED

Seating Arrangement

Comments

Occasion ______________________ *Date* ______________

Theme ______________________ *Time* ______________

MENU & BEVERAGES	LIST	SERVING PIECES	LIST	SHOPPING LIST

TABLE SETTING & DECORATIONS	LIST	MASTER LIST	LIST	
CHINA		INVITATIONS		
SILVER		FOOD		
CRYSTAL		BEVERAGES		
LINENS		WINES/LIQUORS		
CENTERPIECE/CANDLES		FLOWERS		
DECORATIONS		GAMES/ENTERTAINMENT		
OTHER		RENTAL/SERVICES		

Guest List	ACCEPTED	DECLINED	Guest List	ACCEPTED	DECLINED

Seating Arrangement

Comments

Occasion ____________________ *Date* ______________

Theme ____________________ *Time* ______________

MENU & BEVERAGES	LIST	SERVING PIECES	LIST	SHOPPING LIST

TABLE SETTING & DECORATIONS	LIST	MASTER LIST	LIST	
CHINA		INVITATIONS		
SILVER		FOOD		
CRYSTAL		BEVERAGES		
LINENS		WINES/LIQUORS		
CENTERPIECE/CANDLES		FLOWERS		
DECORATIONS		GAMES/ENTERTAINMENT		
OTHER		RENTAL/SERVICES		

Guest List	ACCEPTED	DECLINED	Guest List	ACCEPTED	DECLINED

Seating Arrangement

Comments

Occasion ______________________ *Date* ______________

Theme ______________________ *Time* ______________

MENU & BEVERAGES	LIST	SERVING PIECES	LIST	SHOPPING LIST

TABLE SETTING & DECORATIONS	LIST	MASTER LIST	LIST	
CHINA		INVITATIONS		
SILVER		FOOD		
CRYSTAL		BEVERAGES		
LINENS		WINES/LIQUORS		
CENTERPIECE/CANDLES		FLOWERS		
DECORATIONS		GAMES/ENTERTAINMENT		
OTHER		RENTAL/SERVICES		

Guest List	ACCEPTED	DECLINED	Guest List	ACCEPTED	DECLINED

Seating Arrangement

Comments

Occasion ______________________ *Date* ______________

Theme ______________________ *Time* ______________

MENU & BEVERAGES	LIST	SERVING PIECES	LIST	SHOPPING LIST

TABLE SETTING & DECORATIONS	LIST	MASTER LIST	LIST	
CHINA		INVITATIONS		
SILVER		FOOD		
CRYSTAL		BEVERAGES		
LINENS		WINES/LIQUORS		
CENTERPIECE/CANDLES		FLOWERS		
DECORATIONS		GAMES/ENTERTAINMENT		
OTHER		RENTAL/SERVICES		

Guest List	ACCEPTED	DECLINED	Guest List	ACCEPTED	DECLINED

Seating Arrangement

Comments

Occasion ______________________ *Date* ______________

Theme ______________________ *Time* ______________

MENU & BEVERAGES	✓ LIST	SERVING PIECES	✓ LIST	SHOPPING LIST

TABLE SETTING & DECORATIONS	✓ LIST	MASTER LIST	✓ LIST	
CHINA		INVITATIONS		
SILVER		FOOD		
CRYSTAL		BEVERAGES		
LINENS		WINES/LIQUORS		
CENTERPIECE/CANDLES		FLOWERS		
DECORATIONS		GAMES/ENTERTAINMENT		
OTHER		RENTAL/SERVICES		

Guest List	ACCEPTED	DECLINED	Guest List	ACCEPTED	DECLINED

Seating Arrangement

Comments

Occasion ______________________ *Date* ______________

Theme ______________________ *Time* ______________

MENU & BEVERAGES	LIST	SERVING PIECES	LIST	SHOPPING LIST

TABLE SETTING & DECORATIONS	LIST	MASTER LIST	LIST	
CHINA		INVITATIONS		
SILVER		FOOD		
CRYSTAL		BEVERAGES		
LINENS		WINES/LIQUORS		
CENTERPIECE/CANDLES		FLOWERS		
DECORATIONS		GAMES/ENTERTAINMENT		
OTHER		RENTAL/SERVICES		

Guest List	ACCEPTED	DECLINED	Guest List	ACCEPTED	DECLINED

Seating Arrangement

Comments

Occasion ____________________ *Date* ____________

Theme ____________________ *Time* ____________

MENU & BEVERAGES	✓ LIST	SERVING PIECES	✓ LIST	SHOPPING LIST

TABLE SETTING & DECORATIONS	✓ LIST	MASTER LIST	✓ LIST	
CHINA		INVITATIONS		
SILVER		FOOD		
CRYSTAL		BEVERAGES		
LINENS		WINES/LIQUORS		
CENTERPIECE/CANDLES		FLOWERS		
DECORATIONS		GAMES/ENTERTAINMENT		
OTHER		RENTAL/SERVICES		

Guest List

Guest List	ACCEPTED	DECLINED	Guest List	ACCEPTED	DECLINED

Seating Arrangement

Comments

Occasion ______________________ *Date* ______________

Theme ______________________ *Time* ______________

MENU & BEVERAGES	✓ LIST	SERVING PIECES	✓ LIST	SHOPPING LIST

TABLE SETTING & DECORATIONS	✓ LIST	MASTER LIST	✓ LIST	
CHINA		INVITATIONS		
SILVER		FOOD		
CRYSTAL		BEVERAGES		
LINENS		WINES/LIQUORS		
CENTERPIECE/CANDLES		FLOWERS		
DECORATIONS		GAMES/ENTERTAINMENT		
OTHER		RENTAL/SERVICES		

Guest List	ACCEPTED	DECLINED	Guest List	ACCEPTED	DECLINED

Seating Arrangement

Comments

Occasion ______________________ *Date* ______________

Theme ______________________ *Time* ______________

MENU & BEVERAGES	LIST	SERVING PIECES	LIST	SHOPPING LIST

TABLE SETTING & DECORATIONS	LIST	MASTER LIST	LIST
CHINA		INVITATIONS	
SILVER		FOOD	
CRYSTAL		BEVERAGES	
LINENS		WINES/LIQUORS	
CENTERPIECE/CANDLES		FLOWERS	
DECORATIONS		GAMES/ENTERTAINMENT	
OTHER		RENTAL/SERVICES	

Guest List	ACCEPTED	DECLINED	Guest List	ACCEPTED	DECLINED

Seating Arrangement

Comments

Occasion ______________________ *Date* ______________

Theme ______________________ *Time* ______________

MENU & BEVERAGES	✓LIST	SERVING PIECES	✓LIST	SHOPPING LIST

TABLE SETTING & DECORATIONS	✓LIST	MASTER LIST	✓LIST	
CHINA		INVITATIONS		
SILVER		FOOD		
CRYSTAL		BEVERAGES		
LINENS		WINES/LIQUORS		
CENTERPIECE/CANDLES		FLOWERS		
DECORATIONS		GAMES/ENTERTAINMENT		
OTHER		RENTAL/SERVICES		

Guest List	ACCEPTED	DECLINED	Guest List	ACCEPTED	DECLINED

Seating Arrangement

Comments

Occasion ______________ *Date* ______________

Theme ______________ *Time* ______________

MENU & BEVERAGES	LIST	SERVING PIECES	LIST	SHOPPING LIST

TABLE SETTING & DECORATIONS	LIST	MASTER LIST	LIST	
CHINA		INVITATIONS		
SILVER		FOOD		
CRYSTAL		BEVERAGES		
LINENS		WINES/LIQUORS		
CENTERPIECE/CANDLES		FLOWERS		
DECORATIONS		GAMES/ENTERTAINMENT		
OTHER		RENTAL/SERVICES		

Guest List	ACCEPTED	DECLINED	Guest List	ACCEPTED	DECLINED

Seating Arrangement

Comments

Occasion ______________________ *Date* ______________________

Theme ______________________ *Time* ______________________

MENU & BEVERAGES	LIST	SERVING PIECES	LIST	SHOPPING LIST

TABLE SETTING & DECORATIONS	LIST	MASTER LIST	LIST	
CHINA		INVITATIONS		
SILVER		FOOD		
CRYSTAL		BEVERAGES		
LINENS		WINES/LIQUORS		
CENTERPIECE/CANDLES		FLOWERS		
DECORATIONS		GAMES/ENTERTAINMENT		
OTHER		RENTAL/SERVICES		

Guest List	ACCEPTED	DECLINED	Guest List	ACCEPTED	DECLINED

Seating Arrangement

Comments

Occasion ______________________ *Date* ______________

Theme ______________________ *Time* ______________

MENU & BEVERAGES	✓ LIST	SERVING PIECES	✓ LIST	SHOPPING LIST
TABLE SETTING & DECORATIONS	**✓ LIST**	**MASTER LIST**	**✓ LIST**	
CHINA		INVITATIONS		
SILVER		FOOD		
CRYSTAL		BEVERAGES		
LINENS		WINES/LIQUORS		
CENTERPIECE/CANDLES		FLOWERS		
DECORATIONS		GAMES/ENTERTAINMENT		
OTHER		RENTAL/SERVICES		

Notes

Notes

Notes

Notes

Notes

Wine Notes

Wine Notes

Wine Notes

Wine Notes

Dates to Remember

January

February

March

April

May

June

July

August

September

October

November

December

Notes

Notes

Notes

The Guest Directory

A *Guest Directory*

Name	*Address*	*Telephone*

Guest Directory B

Name	*Address*	*Telephone*

C

Guest Directory

Name	Address	Telephone

Guest Directory D

Name	Address	Telephone

E Guest Directory

Name	Address	Telephone

Guest Directory F

Name	Address	Telephone

G

Guest Directory

Name	Address	Telephone

Guest Directory *H*

Name	*Address*	*Telephone*

I *Guest Directory*

Name	*Address*	*Telephone*

Guest Directory

J

Name	Address	Telephone

K Guest Directory

Name	Address	Telephone

Guest Directory *L*

Name	*Address*	*Telephone*

M *Guest Directory*

Name	*Address*	*Telephone*

Guest Directory *N*

Name	*Address*	*Telephone*

O Guest Directory

Name	Address	Telephone

Guest Directory P

Name	Address	Telephone

2 Guest Directory

Name	*Address*	*Telephone*

Guest Directory R

Name	Address	Telephone

S

Guest Directory

Name	*Address*	*Telephone*

Guest Directory T

Name	Address	Telephone

U Guest Directory

Name	Address	Telephone

Guest Directory *V*

Name	*Address*	*Telephone*

W

Guest Directory

Name	Address	Telephone

Guest Directory *X Y*

Name	*Address*	*Telephone*

Z Guest Directory

Name	Address	Telephone

The Service Directory

Service Directory

BAKERIES	ADDRESS	TELEPHONE

FLORISTS	ADDRESS	TELEPHONE

LIQUOR STORES	ADDRESS	TELEPHONE

Service Directory

BARTENDERS	ADDRESS	TELEPHONE

CATERERS	ADDRESS	TELEPHONE

WAITERS/WAITRESSES	ADDRESS	TELEPHONE

Service Directory

RENTALS	ADDRESS	TELEPHONE

OTHER	ADDRESS	TELEPHONE

Notes

Notes

Notes